Preface

In "The New Revelation" the first dawn of the coming change has been described. In "The Vital Message" the sun has risen higher, and one sees more clearly and broadly what our new relations with the Unseen may be. As I look into the future of the human race I am reminded of how once, from amid the bleak chaos of rock and snow at the head of an Alpine pass, I looked down upon the far stretching view of Lombardy, shimmering in the sunshine and extending in one splendid panorama of blue lakes and green rolling hills until it melted into the golden haze which draped the far horizon. Such a promised land is at our very feet which, when we attain it, will make our present civilisation seem barren and uncouth. Already our vanguard is well over the pass. Nothing can now prevent us from reaching that wonderful land which stretches so clearly before those eyes which are opened to see it.

That stimulating writer, V. C. Desertis, has remarked that the Second Coming, which has always been timed to follow Armageddon, may be fulfilled not by a descent of the spiritual to us, but by the ascent of our material plane to the spiritual, and the blending of the two phases of existence. It is, at least, a fascinating speculation. But without so complete an overthrow of the partition walls as this would imply we know enough already to assure ourselves of such a close approximation as will surely deeply modify all our views of science, of religion and of life. What form these changes may take and what the evidence is upon which they will be founded are briefly set forth in this volume.

ARTHUR CONAN DOYLE.
CROWBOROUGH,
July, 1919.

I. The Two Needful Readjustments

It has been our fate, among all the innumerable generations of mankind, to face the most frightful calamity that has ever befallen the world. There is a basic fact which cannot be denied, and should not be overlooked. For a most important deduction must immediately follow from it. That deduction is that we, who have borne the pains, shall also learn the lesson which they were intended to convey. If we do not learn it and proclaim it, then when can it ever be learned and proclaimed, since there can never again be such a spiritual ploughing and harrowing and preparation for the seed? If our souls, wearied and tortured during these dreadful five years of self-sacrifice and suspense, can show no radical changes, then what souls will ever respond to a fresh influx of heavenly inspiration? In that case the state of the human race would indeed be hopeless, and never in all the coming centuries would there be any prospect of improvement.

Why was this tremendous experience forced upon mankind? Surely it is a superficial thinker who imagines that the great Designer of all things has set the whole planet in a ferment, and strained every nation to exhaustion, in order that this or that frontier be moved, or some fresh combination be formed in the kaleidoscope of nations. No, the causes of the convulsion, and its objects, are more profound than that. They are essentially religious, not political. They lie far deeper than the national squabbles of the day. A thousand years hence those national results may matter little, but the religious result will rule the world. That religious result is the reform of the decadent Christianity of to-day, its simplification, its purification, and its reinforcement by the facts of spirit communion and the clear knowledge of what lies beyond the exit-door of death. The shock of the war was meant to rouse us to mental and moral earnestness, to give us the courage to tear away venerable

ARTHUR CONAN DOYLE

THE VITAL MESSAGE

shams, and to force the human race to realise and use the vast new revelation which has been so clearly stated and so abundantly proved, for all who will examine the statements and proofs with an open mind.

Consider the awful condition of the world before this thunder-bolt struck it. Could anyone, tracing back down the centuries and examining the record of the wickedness of man, find anything which could compare with the story of the nations during the last twenty years! Think of the condition of Russia during that time, with her brutal aristocracy and her drunken democracy, her murders on either side, her Siberian horrors, her Jew baitings and her corruption. Think of the figure of Leopold of Belgium, an incarnate devil who from motives of greed carried murder and torture through a large section of Africa, and yet was received in every court, and was eventually buried after a panegyric from a Cardinal of the Roman Church—a church which had never once raised her voice against his diabolical career. Consider the similar crimes in the Putumayo, where British capitalists, if not guilty of outrage, can at least not be acquitted of having condoned it by their lethargy and trust in local agents. Think of Turkey and the recurrent massacres of her subject races. Think of the heartless grind of the factories everywhere, where work assumed a very different and more unnatural shape than the ancient labour of the fields. Think of the sensuality of many rich, the brutality of many poor, the shallowness of many fashionable, the coldness and deadness of religion, the absence anywhere of any deep, true spiritual impulse. Think, above all, of the organised materialism of Germany, the arrogance, the heartlessness, the negation of everything which one could possibly associate with the living spirit of Christ as evident in the utterances of Catholic Bishops, like Hartmann of Cologne, as in those of Lutheran Pastors. Put all this together and say if the human race has ever presented a more unlovely aspect. When we try to find the brighter spots they are chiefly where civilisation, as apart from religion, has built up necessities for the community, such as hospitals, universities, and organised charities, as conspicuous in Buddhist Japan as in Christian Europe. We cannot deny that there has been much virtue, much gentleness, much spirituality in individuals. But the churches were empty husks, which contained no spiritual food for the human race, and had in the main ceased to influence its actions, save in the direction of soulless forms.

This is not an over-coloured picture. Can we not see, then, what was the inner reason for the war? Can we not understand that it was needful to shake mankind loose from gossip and pink teas, and sword-worship, and Saturday night drunks, and self-seeking politics and theological quibbles—to wake them up and make them realise that they stand upon a narrow knife-edge between two awful eternities, and that, here and now, they have to finish with make-beliefs, and with real earnestness and courage face those truths which have always been palpable where indolence, or cowardice, or vested interests have not obscured the vision. Let us try to appreciate what those truths are and the direction which reform must take. It is the new spiritual developments which predominate in my own thoughts, but there are two other great readjustments which are necessary before they can take their full effect. On the spiritual side I can speak with the force of knowledge from the beyond. On the other two points of reform, I make no such claim.

The first is that in the Bible, which is the foundation of our present religious thought, we have bound together the living and the dead, and the dead has tainted the living. A mummy and an angel are in most unnatural partnership. There can be no clear thinking, and no logical teaching until the old dispensation has been placed on the shelf of the scholar, and removed from the desk of the teacher. It is indeed a wonderful book, in parts the oldest which has come down to us, a book filled with rare knowledge, with history, with poetry, with occultism, with folklore. But it has no connection with modern conceptions of religion. In the main it is actually antagonistic to them. Two contradictory codes have been circulated under one cover, and the result is dire confusion. The one is a scheme depending upon a special tribal God, intensely anthropomorphic and filled with rage, jealousy and revenge. The conception pervades every book of the Old Testament. Even in the psalms, which are perhaps the most spiritual and beautiful section, the psalmist, amid much that is noble, sings of the fearsome things which his God will do to his enemies. "They shall go down alive into hell." There is the keynote of this ancient document—a document which advocates massacre, condones polygamy, accepts slavery, and orders the burning of so-called witches. Its Mosaic provisions have long been laid aside. We do not consider ourselves accursed if we fail to mutilate our bodies, if we eat forbidden dishes, fail to trim our beards, or wear clothes of two materials. But we cannot lay aside the provisions and yet regard the document as divine. No learned quibbles can ever persuade an honest earnest mind that that is right. One may say: "Everyone knows that that is the old dispensation, and is not to be acted upon." It is not true. It is continually acted upon, and always will be so long as it is made part of one sacred book. William the Second acted upon it. His German God which wrought such mischief in the world was the reflection of the dreadful being who ordered that captives be put under the harrow. The cities of Belgium were the reflection of the cities of Moab. Every hard-hearted brute in history, more especially in the religious wars, has found his inspiration in the Old Testament. "Smite and spare not!" "An eye for an eye!", how readily the texts spring to the grim lips of the murderous fanatic. Francis on St. Bartholomew's night, Alva in the Lowlands, Tilly at Magdeburg, Cromwell at Drogheda, the Covenainters at Philliphaugh, the Anabaptists of Munster, and the early Mormons of Utah, all found their murderous impulses fortified from this unholy source. Its red trail runs through history. Even where the New Testament prevails, its teaching must still be dulled and clouded by its sterner neighbour. Let us retain this honoured work of literature. Let us remove the taint which poisons the very spring of our religious thought.

This is, in my opinion, the first clearing which should be made for the more beautiful building to come. The second is less important, as it is a shifting of the point of view, rather than an actual change. It is to be remembered that Christ's life in this world occupied, so far as we can estimate, 33 years, whilst from His arrest to His resurrection was less than a week. Yet the whole Christian system has come to revolve round His death, to the partial exclusion of the beautiful lesson of His life. Far too much weight has been placed upon the one, and far too little upon the other, for the death, beautiful, and indeed perfect, as it was, could be matched by that of many scores of thousands who have died for an idea, while the life, with its consistent record of charity, breadth of mind, unselfishness, courage, reason, and progressiveness, is absolutely unique and superhuman. Even in these abbreviated, translated, and second-hand records we receive an impression such as no other life can give—an impression which fills us with utter reverence. Napoleon, no mean judge of human nature, said of it: "It is different with Christ. Everything about Him astonishes me. His spirit surprises me, and His will confounds me. Between Him and anything of this world there is no possible comparison. He is really a being apart. The nearer I approach Him and the closer I examine Him, the more everything seems above me."

It is this wonderful life, its example and inspiration, which was the real object of the descent of this high spirit on to our planet. If the human race had earnestly centred upon that instead of losing itself in vain dreams of vicarious sacrifices and imaginary falls, with all the mystical and contentious philosophy which has centred round the subject, how very different the level of human culture and happiness would be to-day! Such theories, with their absolute want of reason or morality, have been the main cause why the best minds have been so often alienated from the Christian system and proclaimed themselves materialists. In contemplating what shocked their instincts for truth they have lost that which was both true and beautiful. Christ's death was worthy of His life, and rounded off a perfect career, but it is the life which He has left as the foundation for the permanent religion of mankind. All the religious wars, the private feuds, and the countless miseries of sectarian contention, would have been at least minimised, if not avoided, had the bare example of Christ's life been adopted as the standard of conduct and of religion.

But there are certain other considerations which should have weight when we contemplate this life and its efficacy as an example. One of these is that the very essence of it was that He critically examined religion as He found it, and brought His robust common sense and courage to bear in exposing the shams and in pointing out the better path. THAT is the hall-mark of the true follower of Christ, and not the mute acceptance of doctrines which are, upon the face of them, false and pernicious, because they come to us with some show of authority. What authority have we now, save this very life, which could compare with those Jewish books which were so binding in their force, and so immutably sacred that even the misspellings or pen-slips of the scribe, were most carefully preserved? It is a simple obvious fact that if Christ had been orthodox, and had possessed what is so often praised as a "child-like faith," there could have been no such thing as Christianity. Let reformers who love Him take heart as they consider that they are indeed following in the footsteps of the Master, who has at no time said that the revelation which He brought, and which has been so imperfectly used, is the last which will come to mankind. In our own times an equally great one has been released from the centre of all truth, which will make as deep an impression upon the human race as Christianity, though no predominant figure has yet appeared to enforce its lessons. Such a figure has appeared once when the days were ripe, and I do not doubt that this may occur once more.

One other consideration must be urged. Christ has not given His message in the first person. If He had done so our position would be stronger. It has been repeated by the hearsay and report of earnest but ill-educated men. It speaks much for education in the Roman province of Judea that these fishermen, publicans and others could even read or write. Luke and Paul were, of course, of a higher class, but their information came from their lowly predecessors. Their account is splendidly satisfying in the unity of the general impression which it produces, and the clear drawing of the Master's teaching and character. At the same time it is full of inconsistencies and contradictions upon immaterial matters. For example, the four accounts of the resurrection differ in detail, and there is no orthodox learned lawyer who dutifully accepts all four versions who could not shatter the evidence if he dealt with it in the course of his profession. These details are immaterial to the spirit of the message. It is not common sense to suppose that every item is inspired, or that we have to make no allowance for imperfect reporting, individual convictions, oriental phraseology, or faults of translation. These have, indeed, been admitted by revised versions. In His utterance about the letter and the spirit we could almost believe that Christ had foreseen the plague of texts from which we have suffered, even as He Himself suffered at the hands of the theologians of His day, who then, as now, have been a curse to the world. We were meant to use our reasons and brains in adapting His teaching to the conditions of our altered lives and times. Much depended upon the society and mode of expression which belonged to His era. To suppose in these days that one has literally to give all to the poor, or that a starved English prisoner should literally love his enemy the Kaiser, or that because Christ protested against the lax marriages of His day therefore two spouses who loathe each other should be for ever chained in a life servitude and martyrdom—all these assertions are to travesty His teaching and to take from it that robust quality of common sense which was its main characteristic. To ask what is impossible from human nature is to weaken your appeal when you ask for what is reasonable.

It has already been stated that of the three headings under which reforms are grouped, the exclusion of the old dispensation, the greater attention to Christ's life as compared to His death, and the new spiritual influx which is giving us psychic religion, it is only on the latter that one can quote the authority of the beyond. Here, however, the case is really understated. In regard to the Old Testament I have never seen the matter treated in a spiritual communication. The nature of Christ, however, and His teaching, have been expounded a score of times with some variation of detail, but in the main as reproduced here. Spirits have their individuality of view, and some carry over strong earthly prepossessions which they do not easily shed; but reading many authentic spirit communications one finds that the idea of redemption is hardly ever spoken of, while that of example and influence is for ever insisted upon. In them Christ is the highest spirit known, the son of God, as we all are, but nearer to God, and therefore in a more particular sense His son. He does not, save in most rare and special cases, meet us when we die. Since souls pass over, night and day, at the rate of about 100 a minute, this would seem self-evident. After a time we may be admitted to His presence, to find a most tender, sympathetic and helpful comrade and guide, whose spirit influences all things even when His bodily presence is not visible. This is the general teaching of the other world communications concerning Christ, the gentle, loving and powerful spirit which broods ever over that world which, in all its many spheres, is His special care.

Before passing to the new revelation, its certain proofs and its definite teaching, let us hark back for a moment upon the two points which have already been treated. They are not absolutely vital points. The fresh developments can go on and conquer the world without them. There can be no sudden change in the ancient routine of our religious habits, nor is it possible to conceive that a congress of theologians could take so heroic a step as to tear the Bible in twain, laying one half upon the shelf and one upon the table. Neither is it to be expected that any formal pronouncements could ever be made that the churches have all laid the wrong emphasis upon the story of Christ.

Moral courage will not rise to such a height. But with the spiritual quickening and the greater earnestness which will have their roots in this bloody passion of mankind, many will perceive what is reasonable and true, so that even if the Old Testament should remain, like some obsolete appendix in the animal frame, to mark a lower stage through which development has passed, it will more and more be recognised as a document which has lost all validity and which should no longer be allowed to influence human conduct, save by way of pointing out much which we may avoid. So also with the teaching of Christ, the mystical portions may fade gently away, as the grosser views of eternal punishment have faded within our own lifetime, so that while mankind is hardly aware of the change the heresy of today will become the commonplace of tomorrow. These things will adjust themselves in God's own time.

What is, however, both new and vital are those fresh developments which will now be discussed. In them may be found the signs of how the dry bones may be stirred, and how the mummy may be quickened with the breath of life. With the actual certainty of a definite life after death, and a sure sense of responsibility for our own spiritual development, a responsibility which cannot be put upon any other shoulders, however exalted, but must be borne by each individual for himself, there will come the greatest reinforcement of morality which the human race has ever known. We are on the verge of it now, but our descendants will look upon the past century as the culmination of the dark ages when man lost his trust in God, and was so engrossed in his temporary earth life that he lost all sense of spiritual reality.

II. The Dawning Of The Light

Some sixty years ago that acute thinker Lord Brougham remarked that in the clear sky of scepticism he saw only one small cloud drifting up and that was Modern Spiritualism. It was a curiously inverted simile, for one would surely have expected him to say that in the drifting clouds of scepticism he saw one patch of clear sky, but at least it showed how conscious he was of the coming importance of the movement. Ruskin, too, an equally agile mind, said that his assurance of immortality depended upon the observed facts of Spiritualism. Scores, and indeed hundreds, of famous names could be quoted who have subscribed the same statement, and whose support would dignify any cause upon earth. They are the higher peaks who have been the first to catch the light, but the dawn will spread until none are too lowly to share it. Let us turn, therefore, and inspect this movement which is most certainly destined to revolutionise human thought and action as none other has done within the Christian era. We shall look at it both in its strength and in its weakness, for where one is dealing with what one knows to be true one can fearlessly insist upon the whole of the truth.

The movement which is destined to bring vitality to the dead and cold religions has been called "Modern Spiritualism." The "modern" is good, since the thing itself, in one form or another, is as old as history, and has always, however obscured by forms, been the red central glow in the depths of all religious ideas, permeating the Bible from end to end. But the word "Spiritualism" has been so befouled by wicked charlatans, and so cheapened by many a sad incident, that one could almost wish that some such term as "psychic religion" would clear the subject of old prejudices, just as mesmerism, after many years of obloquy, was rapidly accepted when its name was changed to hypnotism. On the other hand, one remembers the sturdy pioneers who have fought under this banner, and who were prepared to risk their careers, their professional success, and even their reputation for sanity, by publicly asserting what they knew to be the truth.

Their brave, unselfish devotion must do something to cleanse the name for which they fought and suffered. It was they who nursed the system which promises to be, not a new religion—it is far too big for that—but part of the common heritage of knowledge shared by the whole human race. Perfected Spiritualism, however, will probably bear about the same relation to the Spiritualism of 1850 as a modern locomotive to the bubbling little kettle which heralded the era of steam. It will end by being rather the proof and basis of all religions than a religion in itself. We have already too many religions—but too few proofs.

Those first manifestations at Hydesville varied in no way from many of which we have record in the past, but the result arising from them differed very much, because, for the first time, it occurred to a human being not merely to listen to inexplicable sounds, and to fear them or marvel at them, but to establish communication with them. John Wesley's father might have done the same more than a century before had the thought occurred to him when he was a witness of the manifestations at Epworth in 1726. It was only when the young Fox girl struck her hands together and cried "Do as I do" that there was instant compliance, and consequent proof of the presence of an INTELLIGENT invisible force, thus differing from all other forces of which we know. The circumstances were humble, and even rather sordid, upon both sides of the veil, human and spirit, yet it was, as time will more and more clearly show, one of the turning points of the world's history, greater far than the fall of thrones or the rout of armies. Some artist of the future will draw the scene —the sitting-room of the wooden, shack-like house, the circle of half-awed and half-critical neighbours, the child clapping her hands with upturned laughing face, the dark corner shadows where these strange new forces seem to lurk —forces often apparent, and now come to stay and to effect the complete revolution of human thought. We may well ask why should such great results arise from such petty sources? So argued the highbrowed philosophers of Greece and Rome when the outspoken Paul, with the fisherman Peter and his half-educated disciples, traversed all their learned theories, and with the help of women, slaves, and schismatic Jews, subverted their ancient creeds. One can but answer that Providence has its own way of attaining its results, and that it seldom conforms to our opinion of what is most appropriate.

We have a larger experience of such phenomena now, and we can define with some accuracy what it was that happened at Hydesville in the year 1848. We know that these matters are governed by law and by conditions as much as any other phenomena of the universe, though at the moment it seemed to the public to be an isolated and irregular outburst. On the one hand, you had a material, earth-bound spirit of a low order of development which needed a physical medium in order to be able to indicate its presence. On the other, you had that rare thing, a good physical medium. The result followed as surely as the flash follows when the electric battery and wire are both properly adjusted. Corresponding experiments, where effect, and cause duly follow, are being worked out at the present moment by Professor Crawford, of Belfast, as detailed in his two recent books, where he shows that there is an actual loss of weight of the medium in exact proportion to the physical phenomenon produced.[1] The whole secret of mediumship on this material side appears to lie in the power, quite independent of oneself, of passively giving up some portion of one's bodily substance for the use of outside influences. Why should some have this power and some not? We do not know—nor do we know why one should have the ear for music and another not. Each is born in us, and each has little connection with our moral natures. At first it was only physical mediumship which was known, and public attention centred upon moving tables, automatic musical instruments, and other crude but obvious examples of outside influence, which were unhappily very easily imitated by rogues. Since then we have learned that there are many forms of mediumship, so different from each other that an expert at one may have no powers at all at the other. The automatic writer, the clairvoyant, the crystal-seer, the trance speaker, the photographic medium, the direct voice medium, and others, are all, when genuine, the manifestations of one force, which runs through varied channels as it did in the gifts ascribed to the disciples. The unhappy outburst of roguery was helped, no doubt, by the need for darkness claimed by the early experimenters—a claim which is by no means essential, since the greatest of all mediums, D. D. Home, was able by the exceptional strength of his powers to dispense with it. At the same time the fact that darkness rather than light, and dryness rather than moisture, are helpful to good results has been abundantly manifested, and points to the physical laws which underlie the phenomena. The observation made long afterwards that wireless telegraphy, another etheric force, acts twice as well by night as by day, may, corroborate the general conclusions of the early Spiritualists, while their assertion that the least harmful light is red light has a suggestive analogy in the experience of the photographer.

There is no space here for the history of the rise and development of the movement. It provoked warm adhesion and fierce opposition from the start. Professor Hare and Horace Greeley were among the educated minority who tested and endorsed its truth. It was disfigured by many grievous incidents, which may explain but does not excuse the perverse opposition which it encountered in so many quarters. This opposition was really largely based upon the absolute materialism of the age, which would not admit that there could exist at the present moment such conditions as might be accepted in the far past. When actually brought in contact with that life beyond the grave which they professed to believe in, these people winced, recoiled, and declared it impossible. The science of the day was also rooted in materialism, and discarded all its own very excellent axioms when it was faced by an entirely new and unexpected proposition. Faraday declared that in approaching a new subject one should make up one's mind a priori as to what is possible and what is not! Huxley said that the messages, EVEN IF TRUE, "interested him no more than the gossip of curates in a cathedral city." Darwin said: "God help us if we are to believe such things." Herbert Spencer declared against it, but had no time to go into it. At the same time all science did not come so badly out of the ordeal. As already mentioned, Professor Hare, of Philadelphia, inventor, among other things, of the oxy-hydrogen blow-pipe, was the first man of note who had the moral courage, after considerable personal investigation, to declare that these new and strange developments were true. He was followed by many medical men, both in America and in Britain, including Dr. Elliotson, one of the leaders of free thought in this country. Professor Crookes, the most rising chemist in Europe, Dr. Russel Wallace the great naturalist, Varley the electrician, Flammarion the French astronomer, and many others, risked their scientific reputations in their brave assertions of the truth. These men were not credulous fools. They saw and deplored the existence of frauds. Crookes' letters upon the subject are still extant. In very many cases it was the Spiritualists themselves who exposed the frauds. They laughed, as the public laughed, at the sham Shakespeares and vulgar Caesars who figured in certain seance rooms. They deprecated also the low moral tone which would turn such powers to prophecies about the issue of a race or the success of a speculation. But they had that broader vision and sense of proportion which assured them that behind all these follies and frauds there lay a mass of solid evidence which could not be shaken, though like all evidence, it had to be examined before it could be appreciated. They were not such simpletons as to be driven away from a great truth because there are some dishonest camp followers who hang upon its skirts. A great centre of proof and of inspiration lay during those early days in Mr. D. D. Home, a Scottish-American, who possessed powers which make him one of the most remarkable personalities of whom we have any record. Home's life, written by his second wife, is a book which deserves very careful reading. This man, who in some aspects was more than a man, was before the public for nearly thirty years. During that time he never received payment for his services, and was always ready, to put himself at the disposal of any bona-fide and reasonable enquirer. His phenomena were produced in full light, and it was immaterial to him whether the sittings were in his own rooms or in those of his friends. So high were his principles that upon one occasion, though he was a man of moderate means and less than moderate health, he refused the princely fee of two thousand pounds offered for a single sitting by the Union Circle in Paris. As to his powers, they seem to have included every form of mediumship in the highest degree—self-levitation, as witnessed by hundreds of credible witnesses; the handling of fire, with the power of conferring like immunity upon others; the movement without human touch of heavy objects; the visible materialisation of spirits; miracles of healing; and messages from the dead, such as that which converted the hard-headed Scot, Robert Chambers, when Home repeated to him the actual dying words of his young daughter. All this came from a man of so sweet a nature and of so charitable a disposition, that the union of all qualities would seem almost to justify those who, to Home's great embarrassment, were prepared to place him upon a pedestal above humanity.

The genuineness of his psychic powers has never been seriously questioned, and was as well recognised in Rome and Paris as in London. One incident only darkened his career, and it, was one in which he was blameless, as anyone who carefully weighs the evidence must admit. I allude to the action taken against him by Mrs. Lyon, who, after adopting him as her son and settling a large sum of money upon him, endeavoured to regain, and did regain, this money by her unsupported assertion that he had persuaded her illicitly to make him the allowance. The facts of his life are, in my judgment, ample proof of the truth of the Spiritualist position, if no other proof at all had been available. It is to be remarked in the career of this entirely honest and unvenal medium that he had periods in his life when his powers deserted him completely, that he could foresee these lapses, and that, being honest and unvenal, he simply abstained from all attempts until the power returned. It is this intermittent character of the gift which is, in my opinion, responsible for cases when a medium who has passed the most rigid tests upon certain occasions is afterwards detected in simulating, very clumsily, the results which he had once successfully accomplished. The real power having failed, he has not the moral courage to admit it, nor the self-denial to forego his fee which he endeavours to earn by a travesty of what was once genuine. Such an explanation would cover some facts which otherwise are hard to reconcile. We must also admit that some mediums are extremely irresponsible and feather-headed people. A friend of mine, who sat with Eusapia Palladino, assured me that he saw her cheat in the most childish and bare-faced fashion, and yet immediately afterwards incidents occurred which were absolutely beyond any, normal powers to produce. Apart from Home, another episode which marks a stage in the advance of this movement was the investigation and report by the Dialectical Society in the year 1869. This body was composed of men of various learned professions who gathered together to investigate the alleged facts, and ended by reporting that they really WERE facts. They were unbiased, and their conclusions were founded upon results which were very soberly set forth in their report, a most convincing document which, even now in 1919, after the lapse of fifty years, is far more intelligent than the greater part of current opinion upon this subject. None the less, it was greeted by a chorus of ridicule by the ignorant Press of that day, who, if the same men had come to the opposite conclusion in spite of the evidence, would have been ready to hail their verdict as the undoubted end of a pernicious movement. In the early days, about 1863, a book was written by Mrs. de Morgan, the wife of the well-known mathematician Professor de Morgan, entitled "From Matter to Spirit." There is a sympathetic preface by the husband. The book is still well worth reading, for it is a question whether anyone has shown greater brain power in treating the subject. In it the prophecy is made that as the movement develops the more material phenomena will decrease and their place be taken by the more spiritual, such as automatic writing. This forecast has been fulfilled, for though physical mediums still exist the other more subtle forms greatly predominate, and call for far more discriminating criticism in judging their value and their truth. Two very convincing forms of mediumship, the direct voice and spirit photography, have also become prominent. Each of these presents such proof that it is impossible for the sceptic to face them, and he can only avoid them by ignoring them.

In the case of the direct voice one of the leading exponents is Mrs. French, an amateur medium in America, whose work is described both by Mr. Funk and Mr. Randall. She is a frail elderly lady, yet in her presence the most masculine and robust voices make communications, even when her own mouth is covered. I have myself investigated the direct voice in the case of four different mediums, two of them amateurs, and can have no doubt of the reality of the voices, and that they are not the effect of ventriloquism. I was more struck by the failures than by the successes, and cannot easily forget the passionate pantings with which some entity strove hard to reveal his identity to me, but without success. One of these mediums was tested afterwards by having the mouth filled with coloured water, but the voice continued as before. As to spirit photography, the most successful results are obtained by the Crewe circle in England, under the mediumship of Mr. Hope and Mrs. Buxton.[2] I have seen scores of these photographs, which in several cases reproduce exact images of the dead which do not correspond with any pictures of them taken during life. I have seen father, mother, and dead soldier son, all taken together with the dead son looking far the happier and not the least substantial of the three. It is in these varied forms of proof that the impregnable strength of the evidence lies, for how absurd do explanations of telepathy, unconscious cerebration or cosmic memory become when faced by such phenomena as spirit photography, materialisation, or the direct voice. Only one hypothesis can cover every branch of these manifestations, and that is the system of extraneous life and action which has always, for seventy years, held the field for any reasonable mind which had impartially considered the facts. I have spoken of the need for careful and cool-headed analysis in judging the evidence where automatic writing is concerned. One is bound to exclude spirit explanations until all natural ones have been exhausted, though I do not include among natural ones the extreme claims of far-fetched telepathy such as that another person can read in your thoughts things of which you were never yourself aware. Such explanations are not explanations, but mystifications and absurdities, though they seem to have a special attraction for a certain sort of psychical researcher, who is obviously destined to go on researching to the end of time, without ever reaching any conclusion save that of the patience of those who try to follow his reasoning. To give a good example of valid automatic script, chosen out of many which I could quote, I would draw the reader's attention to the facts as to the excavations at Glastonbury, as detailed in "The Gate of Remembrance" by Mr. Bligh Bond. Mr. Bligh Bond, by the way, is not a Spiritualist, but the same cannot be said of the writer of the automatic script, an amateur medium, who was able to indicate the secrets of the buried abbey, which were proved to be correct when the ruins were uncovered. I can truly say that, though I have read much of the old monastic life, it has never been brought home to me so closely as by the messages and descriptions of dear old Brother Johannes, the earth-bound spirit—earthbound by his great love for the old abbey in which he had spent his human life. This book, with its practical sequel, may be quoted as an excellent example of automatic writing at its highest, for what telepathic explanation can cover the detailed description of objects which lie unseen by any human eye? It must be admitted, however, that in automatic writing you are at one end of the telephone, if one may use such a simile, and you have, no assurance as to who is at the other end. You may have wildly false messages suddenly interpolated among truthful ones—messages so detailed in their mendacity that it is impossible to think that they are not deliberately false. When once we have accepted the central fact that spirits change little in essentials when leaving the body, and that in consequence the world is infested by many low and mischievous types, one can understand that these untoward incidents are rather a confirmation of Spiritualism than an argument against it. Personally I have received and have been deceived by several such messages. At the same time I can say that after an experience of thirty years of such com-munications I have never known a blasphemous, an obscene or an unkind sentence come through. I admit, however, that I have heard of such cases. Like attracts like, and one should know one's human company before one joins in such intimate and reverent rites. In clairvoyance the same sudden inexplicable deceptions appear. I have closely followed the work of one female medium, a professional, whose results are so extraordinarily good that in a favourable case she will give the full names of the deceased as well as the most definite and convincing test messages. Yet among this splendid series of results I have notes of several in which she was a complete failure and absolutely wrong upon essentials. How can this be explained? We can only answer that conditions were obviously not propitious, but why or how are among the many problems of the future. It is a profound and most complicated subject, however easily it may be settled by the "ridiculous nonsense" school of critics. I look at the row of books upon the left of my desk as I write—ninety-six solid volumes, many of them annotated and well thumbed, and yet I know that I am like a child wading ankle deep in the margin of an illimitable ocean. But this, at least, I have very clearly realised, that the ocean is there and that the margin is part of it, and that down that shelving shore the human race is destined to move slowly to deeper waters. In the next chapter, I will endeavour to show what is the purpose of the Creator in this strange revelation of new intelligent forces impinging upon our planet. It is this view of the question which must justify the claim that this movement, so long the subject of sneers and ridicule, is absolutely the most important development in the whole history of the human race, so important that, if we could conceive one single man discovering and publishing it, he would rank before Christopher Columbus as a discoverer of new worlds, before Paul as a teacher of new religious truths, and before Isaac Newton as a student of the laws of the Universe.

Before opening up this subject there is one consideration which should have due weight, and yet seems continually to be overlooked. The differences between various sects are a very small thing as compared to the great eternal duel between materialism and the spiritual view of the Universe. That is the real fight. It is a fight in which the Churches championed the anti-material view, but they have done it so unintelligently, and have been continually placed in such false positions, that they have always been losing. Since the days of Hume and Voltaire and Gibbon the fight has slowly but steadily rolled in favour of the attack. Then came

Darwin, showing with apparent truth, that man has never fallen but always risen. This cut deep into the philosophy of orthodoxy, and it is folly to deny it. Then again came the so-called "Higher Criticism," showing alleged flaws and cracks in the very foundations. All this time the churches were yielding ground, and every retreat gave a fresh jumping-off place for a new assault. It has gone so far that at the present moment a very large section of the people of this country, rich and poor, are out of all sympathy not only with the churches but with the whole Spiritual view. Now, we intervene with our positive knowledge and actual proof—an ally so powerful that we are capable of turning the whole tide of battle and rolling it back for ever against materialism. We can say: "We will meet you on your own ground and show you by material and scientific tests that the soul and personality survive." That is the aim of Psychic Science, and it has been fully attained. It means an end to materialism for ever. And yet this movement, this Spiritual movement, is hooted at and reviled by Rome, by Canterbury and even by Little Bethel, each of them for once acting in concert, and including in their battle line such strange allies as the Scientific Agnostics and the militant Free-thinkers. Father Vaughan and the Bishop of London, the Rev. F. B. Meyer and Mr. Clodd, "The Church Times" and "The Freethinker," are united in battle, though they fight with very different battle cries, the one declaring that the thing is of the devil, while the other is equally clear that it does not exist at all. The opposition of the materialists is absolutely intelligent since it is clear that any man who has spent his life in saying "No" to all extramundane forces is, indeed, in a pitiable position when, after many years, he has to recognise that his whole philosophy is built upon sand and that "Yes" was the answer from the beginning. But as to the religious bodies, what words can express their stupidity and want of all proportion in not running halfway and more to meet the greatest ally who has ever intervened to change their defeat into victory?

What gifts this all-powerful ally brings with him, and what are the terms of his alliance, will now be considered.

III. The Great Argument

The physical basis of all psychic belief is that the soul is a complete duplicate of the body, resembling it in the smallest particular, although constructed in some far more tenuous material. In ordinary conditions these two bodies are intermingled so that the identity of the finer one is entirely obscured. At death, however, and under certain conditions in the course of life, the two divide and can be seen separately. Death differs from the conditions of separation before death in that there is a complete break between the two bodies, and life is carried on entirely by the lighter of the two, while the heavier, like a cocoon from which the living occupant has escaped, degenerates and disappears, the world burying the cocoon with much solemnity by taking little pains to ascertain what has become of its nobler contents. It is a vain thing to urge that science has not admitted this contention, and that the statement is pure dogmatism. The science which has not examined the facts has, it is true, not admitted the contention, but its opinion is manifestly worthless, or at the best of less weight than that of the humblest student of psychic phenomena. The real science which has examined the facts is the only valid authority, and it is practically unanimous. I have made personal appeals to at least one great leader of science to examine the facts, however superficially, without any success, while Sir William Crookes appealed to Sir George Stokes, the Secretary of the Royal Society, one of the most bitter opponents of the movement, to come down to his laboratory and see the psychic force at work, but he took no notice. What weight has science of that sort? It can only be compared to that theological prejudice which caused the Ecclesiastics in the days of Galileo to refuse to look through the telescope which he held out to them.

It is possible to write down the names of fifty professors in great seats of learning who have examined and endorsed these facts, and the list would include many of the greatest intellects which the world has produced in our time —Flammarion and Lombroso, Charles Richet and Russel Wallace, Willie Reichel, Myers, Zollner, James, Lodge, and Crookes. Therefore the facts HAVE been endorsed by the only science that has the right to express an opinion. I have never, in my thirty years of experience, known one single scientific man who went thoroughly into this matter and did not end by accepting the Spiritual solution. Such may exist, but I repeat that I have never heard of him. Let us, then, with confidence examine this matter of the "spiritual body," to use the term made classical by Saint Paul. There are many signs in his writings that Paul was deeply versed in psychic matters, and one of these is his exact definition of the natural and spiritual bodies in the service which is the final farewell to life of every Christian. Paul picked his words, and if he had meant that man consisted of a natural body and a spirit he would have said so. When he said "a spiritual body" he meant a body which contained the spirit and yet was distinct from the ordinary natural body. That is exactly what psychic science has now shown to be true.

When a man has taken hashish or certain other drugs, he not infrequently has the experience that he is standing or floating beside his own body, which he can see stretched senseless upon the couch. So also under anaesthetics, particularly under laughing gas, many people are conscious of a detachment from their bodies, and of experiences at a distance. I have myself seen very clearly my wife and children inside a cab while I was senseless in the dentist's chair. Again, when a man is fainting or dying, and his system in an unstable condition, it is asserted in very many definite instances that he can, and does, manifest himself to others at a distance. These phantasms of the living, which have been so carefully explored and docketed by Messrs. Myers and Gurney, ran into hundreds of cases. Some people claim that by an effort of will they can, after going to sleep, propel their own doubles in the direction which they desire, and visit those whom they wish to see. Thus there is a great volume of evidence—how great no man can say who has not spent diligent years in exploring it—which vouches for the existence of this finer body containing the precious jewels of the mind and spirit, and leaving only gross confused animal functions in its heavier companion.

Mr. Funk, who is a critical student of psychic phenomena, and also the joint compiler of the standard American dictionary, narrates a story in point which could be matched from other sources. He tells of an American doctor of his acquaintance, and he vouches personally for the truth of the incident. This doctor, in the course of a cataleptic seizure in Florida, was aware that he had left his body, which he saw lying beside him. He had none the less preserved his figure and his identity. The thought of some friend at a distance came into his mind, and after an appreciable interval he found himself in that friend's room, half way across the continent. He saw his friend, and was conscious that his friend saw him. He afterwards returned to his own room, stood beside his own senseless body, argued within himself whether he should re-occupy it or not, and finally, duty overcoming inclination, he merged his two frames together and continued his life. A letter from him to his friend explaining matters crossed a letter from the friend, in which he told how he also had been aware of his presence. The incident is narrated in detail in Mr. Funk's "Psychic Riddle."

I do not understand how any man can examine the many instances coming from various angles of approach without recognising that there really is a second body of this sort, which incidentally goes far to account for all stories, sacred or profane, of ghosts, apparitions and visions. Now, what is this second body, and how does it fit into modern religious revelation?

What it is, is a difficult question, and yet when science and imagination unite, as Tyndall said they should unite, to throw a searchlight into the unknown, they may produce a beam sufficient to outline vaguely what will become clearer with the future advance of our race. Science has demonstrated that while ether pervades everything the ether which is actually in a body is different from the ether outside it. "Bound" ether is the name given to this, which Fresnel and others have shown to be denser. Now, if this fact be applied to the human body, the result would be that, if all that is visible of that body were removed, there would still remain a complete and absolute mould of the body, formed in bound ether which would be different from the ether around it. This argument is more solid than mere speculation, and it shows that even the soul may come to be defined in terms of matter and is not altogether "such stuff as dreams are made of."

It has been shown that there is some good evidence for the existence of this second body apart from psychic religion, but to those who have examined that religion it is the centre of the whole system, sufficiently real to be recognised by clairvoyants, to be heard by clairaudients, and even to make an exact impression upon a photographic plate. Of the latter phenomenon, of which I have had some very particular opportunities of judging, I have no more doubt than I have of the ordinary photography of commerce. It had already been shown by the astronomers that the sensitized plate is a more delicate recording instrument than the human retina, and that it can show stars upon a long exposure which the eye has never seen. It would appear that the spirit world is really so near to us that a very little extra help under correct conditions of mediumship will make all the difference. Thus the plate, instead of the eye, may bring the loved face within the range of vision, while the trumpet, acting as a megaphone, may bring back the familiar voice where the spirit whisper with no mechanical aid was still inaudible. So loud may the latter phenomenon be that in one case, of which I have the record, the dead man's dog was so excited at hearing once more his master's voice that he broke his chain, and deeply scarred the outside of the seance room door in his efforts to force an entrance.

Now, having said so much of the spirit body, and having indicated that its presence is not vouched for by only one line of evidence or school of thought, let us turn to what happens at the time of death, according to the observation of clairvoyants on this side and the posthumous accounts of the dead upon the other. It is exactly what we should expect to happen, granted the double identity. In a painless and natural process the lighter disengages itself from the heavier, and slowly draws itself off until it stands with the same mind, the same emotions, and an exactly similar body, beside the couch of death, aware of those around and yet unable to make them aware of it, save where that finer spiritual eyesight called clairvoyance exists. How, we may well ask, can it see without the natural organs? How did the hashish victim see his own unconscious body? How did the Florida doctor see his friend? There is a power of perception in the spiritual body which does give the power. We can say no more. To the clairvoyant the new spirit seems like a filmy outline. To the ordinary man it is invisible. To another spirit it would, no doubt, seem as normal and substantial as we appear to each other. There is some evidence that it refines with time, and is therefore nearer to the material at the moment of death or closely after it, than after a lapse of months or years. Hence, it is that apparitions of the dead are most clear and most common about the time of death, and hence also, no doubt, the fact that the cataleptic physician already quoted was seen and recognised by his friend. The meshes of his ether, if the phrase be permitted, were still heavy with the matter from which they had only just been disentangled.

Having disengaged itself from grosser matter, what happens to this spirit body, the precious bark which bears our all in all upon this voyage into unknown seas? Very many accounts have come back to us, verbal and written, detailing the experiences of those who have passed on. The verbal are by trance mediums, whose utterances appear to be controlled by outside intelligences. The written from automatic writers whose script is produced in the same way. At these words the critic naturally and reasonably shies, with a "What nonsense! How can you control the statement of this medium who is consciously or unconsciously pretending to inspiration?" This is a healthy scepticism, and should animate every experimenter who tests a new medium. The proofs must lie in the communication itself. If they are not present, then, as always, we must accept natural rather than unknown explanations. But they are continually present, and in such obvious forms that no one can deny them. There is a certain professional medium to whom I have sent many, mothers who were in need of consolation. I always ask the applicants to report the result to me, and I have their letters of surprise and gratitude before me as I write. "Thank you for this beautiful and interesting experience. She did not make a single mistake about their names, and everything she said was correct." In this case there was a rift between husband and wife before death, but the medium was able, unaided, to explain and clear up the whole matter, mentioning the correct circumstances, and names of everyone concerned, and showing the reasons for the non-arrival of certain letters, which had been the cause of the misunderstanding. The next case was also one of husband and wife, but it is the husband who is the survivor. He says: "It was a most successful sitting. Among other things, I addressed a remark in Danish to my wife (who is a Danish girl), and the answer came back in English without the least hesitation." The next case was again of a man who had lost a very dear male friend. "I have had the most wonderful results with Mrs. —— to-day. I cannot tell you the joy it has been to me. Many grateful thanks for your help." The next one says: "Mrs. —— was simply wonderful. If only more people knew, what agony they would be spared." In this case the wife got in touch with the husband, and the medium mentioned correctly five dead relatives who were in his company. The next is a case of mother and son. "I saw Mrs. —— to-day, and obtained very wonderful results. She told me nearly everything quite correctly—a very few mistakes." The next is similar. "We were quite successful. My boy even reminded me of something that only he and I knew." Says another: "My boy reminded me of the day when he sowed turnip seed upon the lawn. Only he could have known of this." These are fair samples of the letters, of which I hold a large number. They are from people who present themselves from among the millions living in London, or the provinces, and about whose affairs the medium had no possible normal way of knowing. Of all the very numerous cases which I have sent to this medium I have only had a few which have been complete failures. On quoting my results to Sir Oliver Lodge, he remarked that his own experience with another medium had been almost identical. It is no exaggeration to say that our British telephone systems would probably give a larger proportion of useless calls. How is any critic to get beyond these facts save by ignoring or misrepresenting them? Healthy, scepticism is the basis of all accurate observation, but there comes a time when incredulity means either culpable ignorance or else imbecility, and this time has been long past in the matter of spirit intercourse.

In my own case, this medium mentioned correctly the first name of a lady who had died in our house, gave several very characteristic messages from her, described the only two dogs which we have ever kept, and ended by saying that a young officer was holding up a gold coin by which I would recognise him. I had lost my brother-in-law, an army doctor, in the war, and I had given him a spade guinea for his first fee, which he always wore on his chain. There were not more than two or three close relatives who knew about this incident, so that the test was a particularly good one. She made no incorrect statements, though some were vague. After I had revealed the identity of this medium several pressmen attempted to have test seances with her—a test seance being, in most cases, a seance which begins by breaking every psychic condition and making success most improbable. One of these gentlemen, Mr. Ulyss Rogers, had very fair results. Another sent from "Truth" had complete failure. It must be understood that these powers do not work from the medium, but through the medium, and that the forces in the beyond have not the least sympathy with a smart young pressman in search of clever copy, while they have a very different feeling to a bereaved mother who prays with all her broken heart that some assurance may be given her that the child of her love is not gone from her for ever. When this fact is mastered, and it is understood that "Stand and deliver" methods only excite gentle derision on the other side, we shall find some more intelligent manner of putting things of the spirit to the proof.[3]

I have dwelt upon these results, which could be matched by other mediums, to show that we have solid and certain reasons to say that the verbal reports are not from the mediums themselves. Readers of Arthur Hill's "Psychical Investigations" will find many even more convincing cases. So in the written communications, I have in a previous paper pointed to the "Gate of Remembrance" case, but there is a great mass of material which proves that, in spite of mistakes and failures, there really is a channel of communication, fitful and evasive sometimes, but entirely beyond coincidence or fraud. These, then, are the usual means by which we receive psychic messages, though table tilting, ouija boards, glasses upon a smooth surface, or anything which can be moved by the vital animal-magnetic force already discussed will equally serve the purpose. Often information is conveyed orally or by writing which could not have been known to anyone concerned. Mr. Wilkinson has given details of the case where his dead son drew attention to the fact that a curio (a coin bent by a bullet) had been overlooked among his effects. Sir William Barrett has narrated how a young officer sent a message leaving a pearl tie-pin to a friend. No one knew that such a pin existed, but it was found among his things. The death of Sir Hugh Lane was given at a private seance in Dublin before the details of the Lusitania disaster had been published.[4] On that morning we ourselves, in a small seance, got the message "It is terrible, terrible, and will greatly affect the war," at a time when we were convinced that no great loss of life could have occurred. Such examples are very numerous, and are only quoted here to show how impossible it is to invoke telepathy as the origin of such messages. There is only one explanation which covers the facts. They are what they say they are, messages from those who have passed on, from the spiritual body which was seen to rise from the deathbed, which has been so often photographed, which pervades all religion in every age, and which has been able, under proper circumstances, to materialise back into a temporary solidity so that it could walk and talk like a mortal, whether in Jerusalem two thousand years ago, or in the laboratory of Mr. Crookes, in Mornington Road, London.

Let us for a moment examine the facts in this Crookes' episode. A small book exists which describes them, though it is not as accessible as it should be. In these wonderful experiments, which extended over several years, Miss Florrie Cook, who was a young lady of from 16 to 18 years of age, was repeatedly confined in Prof. Crookes' study, the door being locked on the inside. Here she lay unconscious upon a couch. The spectators assembled in the laboratory, which was separated by a curtained opening from the study. After a short interval, through this opening there emerged a lady who was in all ways different from Miss Cook. She gave her earth name as Katie King, and she proclaimed herself to be a materialised spirit, whose mission it was to carry the knowledge of immortality to mortals.

She was of great beauty of face, figure, and manner. She was four and a half inches taller than Miss Cook, fair, whereas the latter was dark, and as different from her as one woman could be from another. Her pulse rate was markedly slower. She became for the time entirely one of the company, walking about, addressing each person present, and taking delight in the children. She made no objection to photography or any other test. Forty-eight photographs of different degrees of excellence were made of her. She was seen at the same time as the medium on several occasions. Finally she departed, saying that her mission was over and that she had other work to do. When she vanished materialism should have vanished also, if mankind had taken adequate notice of the facts. Now, what can the fair-minded inquirer say to such a story as that—one of many, but for the moment we are concentrating upon it? Was Mr. Crookes a blasphemous liar? But there were very many witnesses, as many sometimes as eight at a single sitting. And there are the photographs which include Miss Cook and show that the two women were quite different. Was he honestly mistaken? But that is inconceivable. Read the original narrative and see if you can find any solution save that it is true. If a man can read that sober, cautious statement and not be convinced, then assuredly his brain, is out of gear. Finally, ask yourself whether any religious manifestation in the world has had anything like the absolute proof which lies in this one. Cannot the orthodox see that instead of combating such a story, or talking nonsense about devils, they should hail that which is indeed the final answer to that materialism which is their really dangerous enemy. Even as I write, my eye falls upon a letter on my desk from an officer who had lost all faith in immortality and become an absolute materialist. "I came to dread my return home, for I cannot stand hypocrisy, and I knew well my attitude would cause some members of my family deep grief. Your book has now brought me untold comfort, and I can face the future cheerfully." Are these fruits from the Devil's tree, you timid orthodox critic?

Having then got in touch with our dead, we proceed, naturally, to ask them how it is with them, and under what conditions they exist. It is a very vital question, since what has befallen them yesterday will surely befall us to-morrow. But the answer is tidings of great joy. Of the new vital message to humanity nothing is more important than that. It rolls away all those horrible man-bred fears and fancies, founded upon morbid imaginations and the wild phrases of the oriental. We come upon what is sane, what is moderate, what is reasonable, what is consistent with gradual evolution and with the benevolence of God. Were there ever any conscious blasphemers upon earth who have insulted the Deity so deeply as those extremists, be they Calvinist, Roman Catholic, Anglican, or Jew, who pictured with their distorted minds an implacable torturer as the Ruler of the Universe!

The truth of what is told us as to the life beyond can in its very nature never be absolutely established. It is far nearer to complete proof, however, than any religious revelation which has ever preceded it. We have the fact that these accounts are mixed up with others concerning our present life which are often absolutely true. If a spirit can tell the truth about our sphere, it is difficult to suppose that he is entirely false about his own. Then, again, there is a very great similarity about such accounts, though their origin may be from people very far apart. Thus though "non-veridical," to use the modern jargon, they do conform to all our canons of evidence. A series of books which have attracted far less attention than they deserve have drawn the coming life in very close detail. These books are not found on railway bookstalls or in popular libraries, but the successive editions through which they pass show that there is a deeper public which gets what it wants in spite of artificial obstacles.

Looking over the list of my reading I find, besides nearly a dozen very interesting and detailed manuscript accounts, such published narratives as "Claude's Book," purporting to come from a young British aviator; "Thy Son Liveth," from an American soldier, "Private Dowding"; "Raymond," from a British soldier; "Do Thoughts Perish?"

which contains accounts from several British soldiers and others; "I Heard a Voice," where a well-known K.C., through the mediumship of his two young daughters, has a very full revelation of the life beyond; "After Death," with the alleged experiences of the famous Miss Julia Ames; "The Seven Purposes," from an American pressman, and many others. They differ much in literary skill and are not all equally impressive, but the point which must strike any impartial mind is the general agreement of these various accounts as to the conditions of spirit life. An examination would show that some of them must have been in the press at the same time, so that they could not have each inspired the other. "Claude's Book" and "Thy Son Liveth" appeared at nearly the same time on different sides of the Atlantic, but they agree very closely. "Raymond" and "Do Thoughts Perish?" must also have been in the press together, but the scheme of things is exactly the same. Surely the agreement of witnesses must here, as in all cases, be accounted as a test of truth. They differ mainly, as it seems to me, when they deal with their own future including speculations as to reincarnation, etc., which may well be as foggy to them as it is to us, or systems of philosophy where again individual opinion is apparent.

Of all these accounts the one which is most deserving of study is "Raymond." This is so because it has been compiled from several famous mediums working independently of each other, and has been checked and chronicled by a man who is not only one of the foremost scientists of the world, and probably the leading intellectual force in Europe, but one who has also had a unique experience of the precautions necessary for the observation of psychic phenomena. The bright and sweet nature of the young soldier upon the other side, and his eagerness to tell of his experience is also a factor which will appeal to those who are already satisfied as to the truth of the communications. For all these reasons it is a most important document—indeed it would be no exaggeration to say that it is one of the most important in recent literature. It is, as I believe, an authentic account of the life in the beyond, and it is often more interesting from its sidelights and reservations than for its actual assertions, though the latter bear the stamp of absolute frankness and sincerity. The compilation is in some ways faulty. Sir Oliver has not always the art of writing so as to be understanded of the people, and his deeper and more weighty thoughts get in the way of the clear utterances of his son. Then again, in his anxiety to be absolutely accurate, Sir Oliver has reproduced the fact that sometimes Raymond is speaking direct, and sometimes the control is reporting what Raymond is saying, so that the same paragraph may turn several times from the first person to the third in a manner which must be utterly unintelligible to those who are not versed in the subject. Sir Oliver will, I am sure, not be offended if I say that, having satisfied his conscience by the present edition, he should now leave it for reference, and put forth a new one which should contain nothing but the words of Raymond and his spirit friends. Such a book, published at a low price, would, I think, have an amazing effect, and get all this new teaching to the spot that God has marked for it—the minds and hearts of the people. So much has been said here about mediumship that perhaps it would be well to consider this curious condition a little more closely. The question of mediumship, what it is and how it acts, is one of the most mysterious in the whole range of science. It is a common objection to say if our dead are there why should we only hear of them through people by no means remarkable for moral or mental gifts, who are often paid for their ministration. It is a plausible argument, and yet when we receive a telegram from a brother in Australia we do not say: "It is strange that Tom should not communicate with me direct, but that the presence of that half-educated fellow in the telegraph office should be necessary." The medium is in truth a mere passive machine, clerk and telegraph in one. Nothing comes FROM him. Every message is THROUGH him. Why he or she should have the power more than anyone else is a very interesting problem. This power may best be defined as the capacity for allowing the bodily powers, physical or mental, to be used by an outside influence. In its higher forms there is temporary extinction of personality and the substitution of some other controlling spirit. At such times the medium may entirely lose consciousness, or he may retain it and be aware of some external experience which has been enjoyed by his own entity while his bodily house has been filled by the temporary tenant. Or the medium may retain consciousness, and with eyes and ears attuned to a higher key than the normal man can attain, he may see and hear what is beyond our senses. Or in writing mediumship, a motor centre of the brain regulating the nerves and muscles of the arm may be controlled while all else seems to be normal. Or it may take the more material form of the exudation of a strange white evanescent dough-like substance called the ectoplasm, which has been frequently photographed by scientific enquirers in different stages of its evolution, and which seems to possess an inherent quality of shaping itself into parts or the whole of a body, beginning in a putty-like mould and ending in a resemblance to perfect human members. Or the ectoplasm, which seems to be an emanation of the medium to the extent that whatever it may weigh is so much subtracted from his substance, may be used as projections or rods which can convey objects or lift weights. A friend, in whose judgment and veracity I have absolute confidence, was present at one of Dr. Crawford's experiments with Kathleen Goligher, who is, it may be remarked, an unpaid medium. My friend touched the column of force, and found it could be felt by the hand though invisible to the eye. It is clear that we are in touch with some entirely new form both of matter and of energy. We know little of the properties of this extraordinary substance save that in its materialising form it seems extremely sensitive to the action of light. A figure built up in it and detached from the medium dissolves in light quicker than a snow image under a tropical sun, so that two successive flash-light photographs would show the one a perfect figure, and the next an amorphous mass. When still attached to the medium the ectoplasm flies back with great force on exposure to light, and, in spite of the laughter of the scoffers, there is none the less good evidence that several mediums have been badly injured by the recoil after a light has suddenly been struck by some amateur detective. Professor Geley has, in his recent experiments, described the ectoplasm as appearing outside the black dress of his medium as if a hoar frost had descended upon her, then coalescing into a continuous sheet of white substance, and oozing down until it formed a sort of apron in front of her.[5] This process he has illustrated by a very complete series of photographs.

These are a few of the properties of mediumship. There are also the beautiful phenomena of the production of lights, and the rarer, but for evidential purposes even more valuable, manifestations of spirit photography. The fact that the photograph does not correspond in many cases with any which existed in life, must surely silence the scoffer, though there is a class of bigoted sceptic who would still be sneering if an Archangel alighted in Trafalgar Square. Mr. Hope and Mrs. Buxton, of Crewe, have brought this phase of mediumship to great perfection, though others have powers in that direction. Indeed, in some cases it is difficult to say who the medium may have been, for in one collective family group which was taken in the ordinary way, and was sent me by a master in a well known public school, the young son who died has appeared in the plate seated between his two little brothers. As to the personality of mediums, they have seemed to me to be very average specimens of the community, neither markedly better nor markedly worse. I know many, and I have never met anything in the least like "Sludge," a poem which Browning might be excused for writing in some crisis of domestic disagreement, but which it was inexcusable to republish since it is admitted to be a concoction, and the exposure described to have been imaginary. The critic often uses the term medium as if it necessarily meant a professional, whereas every investigator has found some of his best results among amateurs. In the two finest seances I ever attended, the psychic, in each case a man of moderate means, was resolutely determined never directly or indirectly to profit by his gift, though it entailed very exhausting physical conditions. I have not heard of a clergyman of any denomination who has attained such a pitch of altruism—nor is it reasonable to expect it. As to professional mediums, Mr. Vout Peters, one of the most famous, is a diligent collector of old books and an authority upon the Elizabethan drama; while Mr. Dickinson, another very remarkable discerner of spirits, who named twenty-four correctly during two meetings held on the same day, is employed in loading canal barges. This man is one gifted clairvoyants in England, though Tom Tyrrell the weaver, Aaron Wilkinson, and others are very marvellous. Tyrrell, who is a man of the Anthony of Padua type, a walking saint, beloved of animals and children, is a figure who might have stepped out of some legend of the church. Thomas, the powerful physical medium, is a working coal miner. Most mediums take their responsibilities very seriously and view their work in a religious light. There is no denying that they are exposed to very particular temptations, for the gift is, as I have explained elsewhere, an intermittent one, and to admit its temporary absence, and so discourage one's clients, needs greater moral principle than all men possess. Another temptation to which several great mediums have succumbed is that of drink. This comes about in a very natural way, for overworking the power leaves them in a state of physical prostration, and the stimulus of alcohol affords a welcome relief, and may tend at last to become a custom and finally a curse. Alcoholism always weakens the moral sense, so that these degenerate mediums yield themselves more readily to fraud, with the result that several who had deservedly won honoured names and met all hostile criticism have, in their later years, been detected in the most contemptible tricks. It is a thousand pities that it should be so, but if the Court of Arches were to give up its secrets, it would be found that tippling and moral degeneration were by no means confined to psychics. At the same time, a psychic is so peculiarly sensitive that I think he or she would always be well advised to be a life long abstainer —as many actually are.

As to the method by which they attain their results they have, when in the trance state, no recollection. In the case of normal clairvoyants and clairaudients, the information comes in different ways. Sometimes it is no more than a strong mental impression which gives a name or an address. Sometimes they say that they see it written up before them. Sometimes the spirit figures seem to call it to them. "They yell it at me," said one.

We need more first-hand accounts of these matters before we can formulate laws.

It has been stated in a previous book by the author, but it will bear repetition, that the use of the seance should, in his opinion, be carefully regulated as well as reverently conducted. Having once satisfied himself of the absolute existence of the unseen world, and of its proximity to our own, the inquirer has got the great gift which psychical investigation can give him, and thenceforth he can regulate his life upon the lines which the teaching from beyond has shown to be the best. There is much force in the criticism that too constant intercourse with the affairs of another world may distract our attention and weaken our powers in dealing with our obvious duties in this one. A seance, with the object of satisfying curiosity or of rousing interest, cannot be an elevating influence, and the mere sensation-monger can make this holy and wonderful thing as base as the over-indulgence in a stimulant. On the other hand, where the seance is used for the purpose of satisfying ourselves as to the condition of those whom we have lost, or of giving comfort to others who crave for a word from beyond, then it is, indeed, a blessed gift from God to be used with moderation and with thankfulness. Our loved ones have their own pleasant tasks in their new surroundings, and though they assure us that they love to clasp the hands which we stretch out to them, we should still have some hesitation in intruding to an unreasonable extent upon the routine of their lives. A word should be said as to that fear of fiends and evil spirits which appears to have so much weight with some of the critics of this subject. When one looks more closely at this emotion it seems somewhat selfish and cowardly. These creatures are in truth our own backward brothers, bound for the same ultimate destination as ourselves, but retarded by causes for which our earth conditions may have been partly responsible. Our pity and sympathy should go out to them, and if they do indeed manifest at a seance, the proper Christian attitude is, as it seems to me, that we should reason with them and pray for them in order to help them upon their difficult way. Those who have treated them in this way have found a very marked difference in the subsequent communications. In Admiral Usborne Moore's "Glimpses of the Next State" there will be found some records of an American circle which devoted itself entirely to missionary work of this sort. There is some reason to believe that there are forms of imperfect development which can be helped more by earthly than by purely spiritual influences, for the reason, perhaps, that they are closer to the material.

In a recent case I was called in to endeavour to check a very noisy entity which frequented an old house in which there were strong reasons to believe that crime had been committed, and also that the criminal was earth-bound. Names were given by the unhappy spirit which proved to be correct, and a cupboard was described, which was duly found, though it had never before been suspected. On getting into touch with the spirit I endeavoured to reason with it and to explain how selfish it was to cause misery to others in order to satisfy any feelings of revenge which it might have carried over from earth life. We then prayed for its welfare, exhorted it to rise higher, and received a very solemn assurance, tilted out at the table, that it would mend its ways. I have very gratifying reports that it has done so, and that all is now quiet in the old house.

Let us now consider the life in the Beyond as it is shown to us by the new revelation.

IV. The Coming World

We come first to the messages which tell us of the life beyond the grave, sent by those who are actually living it. I have already insisted upon the fact that they have three weighty claims to our belief. The one is, that they are accompanied by "signs," in the Biblical sense, in the shape of "miracles" or phenomena. The second is, that in many cases they are accompanied by assertions about this life of ours which prove to be correct, and which are beyond the possible knowledge of the medium after every deduction has been made for telepathy or for unconscious memory. The third is, that they have a remarkable, though not a complete, similarity from whatever source they come.

It may be noted that the differences of opinion become most marked when they deal with their own future, which may well be a matter of speculation to them as to us. Thus, upon the question of reincarnation there is a distinct cleavage, and though I am myself of opinion that the general evidence is against this oriental doctrine, it is none the less an undeniable fact that it has been maintained by some messages which appear in other ways to be authentic, and, therefore, it is necessary to keep one's mind open on the subject.

Before entering upon the substance of the messages I should wish to emphasize the second of these two points, so as to reinforce the reader's confidence in the authenticity of these assertions. To this end I will give a detailed example, with names almost exact. The medium was Mr. Phoenix, of Glasgow, with whom I have myself had some remarkable experiences. The sitter was Mr. Ernest Oaten, the President of the Northern Spiritual Union, a man of the utmost veracity and precision of statement. The dialogue, which came by the direct voice, a trumpet acting as megaphone, ran like this:

The Voice: Good evening, Mr. Oaten. Mr. O.: Good evening. Who are you? The Voice: My name is Mill. You know my father. Mr. O.: No, I don't remember anyone of the name. The Voice: Yes, you were speaking to him the other day. Mr. O.: To be sure. I remember now. I only met him casually. The Voice: I want you to give him a message from me. Mr. O.: What is it? The Voice: Tell him that he was not mistaken at midnight on Tuesday last. Mr. O.: Very good. I will say so. Have you passed long? The Voice: Some time. But our time is different from yours. Mr. O.: What were you? The Voice: A Surgeon. Mr. O.: How did you pass? The Voice: Blown up in a battleship during the war. Mr. O.: Anything more?

The answer was the Gipsy song from "Il Trovatore," very accurately whistled, and then a quick-step. After the latter, the voice said: "That is a test for father."

This reproduction of conversation is not quite verbatim, but gives the condensed essence. Mr. Oaten at once visited Mr. Mill, who was not a Spiritualist, and found that every detail was correct. Young Mill had lost his life as narrated. Mr. Mill, senior, explained that while sitting in his study at midnight on the date named he had heard the Gipsy song from "Il Trovatore," which had been a favourite of his boy's, and being unable to trace the origin of the music, had finally thought that it was a freak of his imagination. The test connected with the quick-step had reference to a tune which the young man used to play upon the piccolo, but which was so rapid that he never could get it right, for which he was chaffed by the family.

I tell this story at length to make the reader realise that when young Mill, and others like him, give such proofs of accuracy, which we can test for ourselves, we are bound to take their assertions very seriously when they deal with the life they are actually leading, though in their very nature we can only check their accounts by comparison with others.

Now let me epitomise what these assertions are. They say that they are exceedingly happy, and that they do not wish to return. They are among the friends whom they had loved and lost, who meet them when they die and continue their careers together. They are very busy on all forms of congenial work. The world in which they find themselves is very much like that which they have quitted, but everything keyed to a higher octave. As in a higher octave the rhythm is the same, and the relation of notes to each other the same, but the total effect different, so it is here. Every earthly thing has its equivalent. Scoffers have guffawed over alcohol and tobacco, but if all things are reproduced it would be a flaw if these were not reproduced also. That they should be abused, as they are here, would, indeed, be evil tidings, but nothing of the sort has been said, and in the much discussed passage in "Raymond," their production was alluded to as though it were an unusual, and in a way a humorous, instance of the resources of the beyond. I wonder how many of the preachers, who have taken advantage of this passage in order to attack the whole new revelation, have remembered that the only other message which ever associated alcohol with the life beyond is that of Christ Himself, when He said: "I will not drink henceforth of this fruit of the vine until that day when I drink it new with you in my Father's kingdom."

This matter is a detail, however, and it is always dangerous to discuss details in a subject which is so enormous, so dimly seen. As the wisest woman I have known remarked to me: "Things may well be surprising over there, for if we had been told the facts of this life before we entered it, we should never have believed it." In its larger issues this happy life to come consists in the development of those gifts which we possess. There is action for the man of action, intellectual work for the thinker, artistic, literary, dramatic and religious for those whose God-given powers lie that way. What we have both in brain and character we carry over with us. No man is too old to learn, for what he learns he keeps. There is no physical side to love and no child-birth, though there is close union between those married people who really love each other, and, generally, there is deep sympathetic friendship and comradeship between the sexes. Every man or woman finds a soul mate sooner or later. The child grows up to the normal, so that the mother who lost a babe of two years old, and dies herself twenty years later finds a grown-up daughter of twenty-two awaiting her coming. Age, which is produced chiefly by the mechanical presence of lime in our arteries, disappears, and the individual reverts to the full normal growth and appearance of completed man—or womanhood. Let no woman mourn her lost beauty, and no man his lost strength or weakening brain. It all awaits them once more upon the other side. Nor is any deformity or bodily weakness there, for all is normal and at its best.

Before leaving this section of the subject, I should say a few more words upon the evidence as it affects the etheric body. This body is a perfect thing. This is a matter of consequence in these days when so many of our heroes have been mutilated in the wars. One cannot mutilate the etheric body, and it remains always intact. The first words uttered by a returning spirit in the recent experience of Dr. Abraham Wallace were "I have got my left arm again." The same applies to all birth marks, deformities, blindness, and other imperfections. None of them are permanent, and all will vanish in that happier life that awaits us. Such is the teaching from the beyond—that a perfect body waits for each.

"But," says the critic, "what then of the clairvoyant descriptions, or the visions where the aged father is seen, clad in the old-fashioned garments of another age, or the grandmother with crinoline and chignon? Are these the habiliments of heaven?" Such visions are not spirits, but they are pictures which are built up before us or shot by spirits into our brains or those of the seer for the purposes of recognition. Hence the grey hair and hence the ancient garb. When a real spirit is indeed seen it comes in another form to this, where the flowing robe, such as has always been traditionally ascribed to the angels, is a vital thing which, by its very colour and texture, proclaims the spiritual condition of the wearer, and is probably a condensation of that aura which surrounds us upon earth.

It is a world of sympathy. Only those who have this tie foregather. The sullen husband, the flighty wife, is no longer there to plague the innocent spouse. All is sweet and peaceful. It is the long rest cure after the nerve strain of life, and before new experiences in the future. The circumstances are homely and familiar. Happy circles live in pleasant homesteads with every amenity of beauty and of music. Beautiful gardens, lovely flowers, green woods, pleasant lakes, domestic pets—all of these things are fully described in the messages of the pioneer travellers who have at last got news back to those who loiter in the old dingy home. There are no poor and no rich. The craftsman may still pursue his craft, but he does it for the joy of his work. Each serves the community as best he can, while from above come higher ministers of grace, the "Angels" of holy writ, to direct and help. Above all, shedding down His atmosphere upon all, broods that great Christ spirit, the very soul of reason, of justice, and of sympathetic understanding, who has the earth sphere, with all its circles, under His very special care. It is a place of joy and laughter. There are games and sports of all sorts, though none which cause pain to lower life. Food and drink in the grosser sense do not exist, but there seem to be pleasures of taste, and this distinction causes some confusion in the messages upon the point.

But above all, brain, energy, character, driving power, if exerted for good, makes a man a leader there as here, while unselfishness, patience and spirituality there, as here, qualify the soul for the higher places, which have often been won by those very tribulations down here which seem so purposeless and so cruel, and are in truth our chances of spiritual quickening and promotion, without which life would have been barren and without profit.

The revelation abolishes the idea of a grotesque hell and of a fantastic heaven, while it substitutes the conception of a gradual rise in the scale of existence without any monstrous change which would turn us in an instant from man to angel or devil. The system, though different from previous ideas, does not, as it seems to me, run counter in any radical fashion to the old beliefs. In ancient maps it was usual for the cartographer to mark blank spaces for the unexplored regions, with some such legend as "here are anthropophagi," or "here are mandrakes," scrawled across them. So in our theology there have been ill-defined areas which have admittedly been left unfilled, for what sane man has ever believed in such a heaven as is depicted in our hymn books, a land of musical idleness and barren monotonous adoration! Thus in furnishing a clearer conception this new system has nothing to supplant. It paints upon a blank sheet.

One may well ask, however, granting that there is evidence for such a life and such a world as has been described, what about those who have not merited such a destination? What do the messages from beyond say about these? And here one cannot be too definite, for there is no use exchanging one dogma for another. One can but give the general purport of such information as has been vouchsafed to us. It is natural that those with whom we come in contact are those whom we may truly call the blessed, for if the thing be approached in a reverent and religious spirit it is those whom we should naturally attract. That there are many less fortunate than themselves is evident from their own constant allusions to that regenerating and elevating missionary work which is among their own functions. They descend apparently and help others to gain that degree of spirituality which fits them for this upper sphere, as a higher student might descend to a lower class in order to bring forward a backward pupil. Such a conception gives point to Christ's remark that there was more joy in heaven over saving one sinner than over ninety-nine just, for if He had spoken of an earthly sinner he would surely have had to become just in this life and so ceased to be a sinner before he had reached Paradise.

It would apply very exactly, however, to a sinner rescued from a lower sphere and brought to a higher one.

When we view sin in the light of modern science, with the tenderness of the modern conscience and with a sense of justice and proportion, it ceases to be that monstrous cloud which darkened the whole vision of the mediaeval theologian. Man has been more harsh with himself than an all-merciful God will ever be. It is true that with all deductions there remains a great residuum which means want of individual effort, conscious weakness of will, and culpable failure of character when the sinner, like Horace, sees and applauds the higher while he follows the lower. But when, on the other hand, one has made allowances—and can our human allowance be as generous as God's?—for the sins which are the inevitable product of early environment, for the sins which are due to hereditary and inborn taint, and to the sins which are due to clear physical causes, then the total of active sin is greatly reduced. Could one, for example, imagine that Providence, all-wise and all-merciful, as every creed proclaims, could punish the unfortunate wretch who hatches criminal thoughts behind the slanting brows of a criminal head? A doctor has but to glance at the cranium to predicate the crime. In its worst forms all crime, from Nero to Jack the Ripper, is the product of absolute lunacy, and those gross national sins to which allusion has been made seem to point to collective national insanity. Surely, then, there is hope that no very terrible inferno is needed to further punish those who have been so afflicted upon earth. Some of our dead have remarked that nothing has surprised them so much as to find who have been chosen for honour, and certainly, without in any way condoning sin, one could well imagine that the man whose organic makeup predisposed him with irresistible force in that direction should, in justice, receive condolence and sympathy. Possibly such a sinner, if he had not sinned so deeply as he might have done, stands higher than the man who was born good, and remained so, but was no better at the end of his life. The one has made some progress and the other has not. But the commonest failing, the one which fills the spiritual hospitals of the other world, and is a temporary bar to the normal happiness of the after-life, is the sin of Tomlinson in Kipling's poem, the commonest of all sins in respectable British circles, the sin of conventionality, of want of conscious effort and develop-ment, of a sluggish spirituality, fatted over by a complacent mind and by the comforts of life. It is the man who is satisfied, the man who refers his salvation to some church or higher power without steady travail of his own soul, who is in deadly danger. All churches are good, Christian or non-Christian, so long as they promote the actual spirit life of the individual, but all are noxious the instant that they allow him to think that by any form of ceremony, or by any fashion of creed, he obtains the least advantage over his neighbour, or can in any way dispense with that personal effort which is the only road to the higher places. This is, of course, as appli-cable to believers in Spiritualism as to any other belief. If it does not show in practice then it is vain. One can get through this life very comfortably following without question in some procession with a venerable leader. But one does not die in a procession. One dies alone. And it is then that one has alone to accept the level gained by the work of life.

And what is the punishment of the undeveloped soul? It is that it should be placed where it WILL develop, and sorrow would seem always to be the forcing ground of souls. That surely is our own experience in life where the insuf-ferably complacent and unsympathetic person softens and mellows into beauty of character and charity of thought, when tried long enough and high enough in the fires of life. The Bible has talked about the "Outer darkness where there is weeping and gnashing of teeth." The influence of the Bible has sometimes been an evil one through our own habit of reading a book of Oriental poetry and treating it as literally as if it were Occidental prose. When an Eastern describes a herd of a thousand camels he talks of camels which are more numerous than the hairs of your head or the stars in the sky. In this spirit of allowance for Eastern expression, one must approach those lurid and terrible descriptions which have darkened the lives of so many imaginative children and sent so many earnest adults into asylums. From all that we learn there are indeed places of outer darkness, but dim as these uncomfortable waiting-rooms may be, they all admit to heaven in the end. That is the final destination of the human race, and it would indeed be a reproach to the Almighty if it were not so. We cannot dogmatise upon this subject of the penal spheres, and yet we have very clear teaching that they are there and that the no-man's-land which separates us from the normal heaven, that third heaven to which St. Paul seems to have been wafted in one short strange experience of his lifetime, is a place which corresponds with the Astral plane of the mystics and with the "outer darkness" of the Bible. Here linger those earth-bound spirits whose worldly interests have clogged them and weighed them down, until every spiritual impulse had vanished; the man whose life has been centred on money, on worldly ambition, or on sensual indulgence. The one-idea'd man will surely be there, if his one idea was not a spiritual one. Nor is it necessary that he should be an evil man, if dear old brother John of Glastonbury, who loved the great Abbey so that he could never detach himself from it, is to be classed among earth-bound spirits. In the most material and pronounced classes of these are the ghosts who impinge very closely upon matter and have been seen so often by those who have no strong psychic sense. It is probable, from what we know of the material laws which govern such matters, that a ghost could never manifest itself if it were alone, that the substance for the manifestation is drawn from the spectator, and that the coldness, raising of hair, and other symptoms of which he complains are caused largely by the sudden drain upon his own vitality. This, however, is to wander into speculation, and far from that correlation of psychic knowledge with religion, which has been the aim of these chapters.

By one of those strange coincidences, which seem to me sometimes to be more than coincidences, I had reached this point in my explanation of the difficult question of the intermediate state, and was myself desiring further enlightenment, when an old book reached me through the post, sent by someone whom I have never met, and in it is the following passage, written by an automatic writer, and in existence since 1880. It makes the matter plain, endorsing what has been said and adding new points.

"Some cannot advance further than the borderland— such as never thought of spirit life and have lived entirely for the earth, its cares and pleasures—even clever men and women, who have lived simply intellectual lives without spirituality. There are many who have misused their opportunities, and are now longing for the time misspent and wishing to recall the earth-life. They will learn that on this side the time can be redeemed, though at much cost. The borderland has many among the restless money-getters of earth, who still haunt the places where they had their hopes and joys. These are often the longest to remain . . . many are not unhappy. They feel the relief to be sufficient to be without their earth bodies. All pass through the borderland, but some hardly perceive it. It is so immediate, and there is no resting there for them. They pass on at once to the refreshment place of which we tell you." The anonymous author, after recording this spirit message, mentions the interesting fact that there is a Christian inscription in the Catacombs which runs: NICEFORUS ANIMA DULCIS IN REFRIGERIO, "Nicephorus, a sweet soul in the refreshment place." One more scrap of evidence that the early Christian scheme of things was very like that of the modern psychic. So much for the borderland, the intermediate condition. The present Christian dogma has no name for it, unless it be that nebulous limbo which is occasionally mentioned, and is usually defined as the place where the souls of the just who died before Christ were detained. The idea of crossing a space before reaching a permanent state on the other side is common to many religions, and took the allegorical form of a river with a ferry-boat among the Romans and Greeks. Continually, one comes on points which make one realise that far back in the world's history there has been a true revelation, which has been blurred and twisted in time. Thus in Dr. Muir's summary of the RIG. VEDA, he says, epitomising the beliefs of the first Aryan conquerors of India: "Before, however, the unborn part" (that is, the etheric body) "can complete its course to the third heaven it has to traverse a vast gulf of darkness, leaving behind on earth all that is evil, and proceeding by the paths the fathers trod, the spirit soars to the realms of eternal light, recovers there his body in a glorified form, and obtains from God a delectable abode and enters upon a more perfect life, which is crowned with the fulfilment of all desires, is passed in the presence of the Gods and employed in the fulfilment of their pleasure." If we substitute "angels" for "Gods" we must admit that the new revelation from modern spirit sources has much in common with the belief of our Aryan fathers. Such, in very condensed form, is the world which is revealed to us by these wonderful messages from the beyond. Is it an unreasonable vision? Is it in any way opposed to just principles? Is it not rather so reasonable that having got the clue we could now see that, given any life at all, this is exactly the line upon which we should expect to move? Nature and evolution are averse from sudden disconnected develop-ments. If a human being has technical, literary, musical, or other tendencies, they are an essential part of his character, and to survive without them would be to lose his identity and to become an entirely different man. They must therefore survive death if personality is to be maintained. But it is no use their surviving unless they can find means of expression, and means of expression seem to require certain material agents, and also a discriminating audience. So also the sense of modesty among civilised races has become part of our very selves, and implies some covering of our forms if personality is to continue. Our desires and sympathies would prompt us to live with those we love, which implies something in the nature of a house, while the human need for mental rest and privacy would predicate the existence of separate rooms. Thus, merely starting from the basis of the continuity of personality one might, even without the revelation from the beyond, have built up some such system by the use of pure reason and deduction.

So far as the existence of this land of happiness goes, it would seem to have been more fully proved than any other religious conception within our knowledge.

It may very reasonably be asked, how far this precise description of life beyond the grave is my own conception, and how far it has been accepted by the greater minds who have studied this subject? I would answer, that it is my own conclusion as gathered from a very large amount of existing testimony, and that in its main lines it has for many years been accepted by those great numbers of silent active workers all over the world, who look upon this matter from a strictly religious point of view. I think that the evidence amply justifies us in this belief. On the other hand, those who have approached this subject with cold and cautious scientific brains, endowed, in many cases, with the strongest prejudices against dogmatic creeds and with very natural fears about the possible re-growth of theological quarrels, have in most cases stopped short of a complete acceptance, declaring that there can be no positive proof upon such matters, and that we may deceive ourselves either by a reflection of our own thoughts or by receiving the impressions of the medium. Professor Zollner, for example, says:

"Science can make no use of the substance of intellectual revelations, but must be guided by observed facts and by the conclusions logically and mathematically uniting them"—a passage which is quoted with approval by Professor Reichel, and would seem to be endorsed by the silence concerning the religious side of the question which is observed by most of our great scientific supporters. It is a point of view which can well be understood, and yet, closely examined, it would appear to be a species of enlarged materialism. To admit, as these observers do, that spirits do return, that they give every proof of being the actual friends whom we have lost, and yet to turn a deaf ear to the messages which they send would seem to be pushing caution to the verge of unreason. To get so far, and yet not to go further, is impossible as a permanent position. If, for example, in Raymond's case we find so many allusions to the small details of his home upon earth, which prove to be surprisingly correct, is it reasonable to put a blue pencil through all he says of the home which he actually inhabits? Long before I had convinced my mind of the truth of things which appeared so grotesque and incredible, I had a long account sent by table tilting about the conditions of life beyond. The details seemed to me impossible and I set them aside, and yet they harmonise, as I now discover, with other revelations. So, too, with the automatic script of Mr. Hubert Wales, which has been described in my previous book. He had tossed it aside into a drawer as being unworthy of serious consideration, and yet it also proved to be in harmony. In neither of these cases was telepathy or the prepossession of the medium a possible explanation. On the whole, I am inclined to think that these doubtful or dissentient scientific men, having their own weighty studies to attend to, have confined their reading and thought to the more objective side of the question, and are not aware of the vast amount of concurrent evidence which appears to give us an exact picture of the life beyond. They despise documents which cannot be proved, and they do not, in my opinion, sufficiently realise that a general agreement of testimony, and the already established character of a witness, are themselves arguments for truth. Some complicate the question by predicating the existence of a fourth dimension in that world, but the term is an absurdity, as are all terms which find no corresponding impression in the human brain. We have mysteries enough to solve without gratuitously introducing fresh ones. When solid passes through solid, it is, surely, simpler to assume that it is done by a dematerialisation, and subsequent reassembly—a process which can, at least, be imagined by the human mind—than to invoke an explanation which itself needs to be explained.

In the next and final chapter I will ask the reader to accompany me in an examination of the New Testament by the light of this psychic knowledge, and to judge how far it makes clear and reasonable much which was obscure and confused.

V. Is It The Second Dawn?

There are many incidents in the New Testament which might be taken as starting points in tracing a close analogy between the phenomenal events which are associated with the early days of Christianity, and those which have perplexed the world in connection with modern Spiritualism. Most of us are prepared to admit that the lasting claims of Christianity upon the human race are due to its own intrinsic teachings, which are quite independent of those wonders which can only have had a use in startling the solid complacence of an unspiritual race, and so directing their attention violently to this new system of thought. Exactly the same may be said of the new revelation. The exhibitions of a force which is beyond human experience and human guidance is but a method of calling attention. To repeat a simile which has been used elsewhere, it is the humble telephone bell which heralds the all-important message. In the case of Christ, the Sermon on the Mount was more than many miracles. In the case of this new development, the messages from beyond are more than any phenomena. A vulgar mind might make Christ's story seem vulgar, if it insisted upon loaves of bread and the bodies of fish. So, also, a vulgar mind may make psychic religion vulgar by insisting upon moving furniture or tambourines in the air. In each case they are crude signs of power, and the essence of the matter lies upon higher planes.

It is stated in the second chapter of the Acts of the Apostles, that they, the Christian leaders, were all "with one accord" in one place. "With one accord" expresses admirably those sympathetic conditions which have always been found, in psychic circles, to be conducive of the best results, and which are so persistently ignored by a certain class of investigators. Then there came "a mighty rushing wind," and afterwards "there appeared cloven tongues like unto fire and it sat upon each of them." Here is a very definite and clear account of a remarkable sequence of phenomena. Now, let us compare with this the results which were obtained by Professor Crookes in his investigation in 1873, after he had taken every possible precaution against fraud which his experience, as an accurate observer and experimenter, could suggest. He says in his published notes: "I have seen luminous points of light darting about, sitting on the heads of different persons" and then again:

"These movements, and, indeed, I may say the same of every class of phenomena, are generally preceded by a peculiar cold air, sometimes amounting to a decided wind. I have had sheets of paper blown about by it. . . ." Now, is it not singular, not merely that the phenomena should be of the same order, but that they should come in exactly the same sequence, the wind first and the lights afterwards? In our ignorance of etheric physics, an ignorance which is now slowly clearing, one can only say that there is some indication here of a general law which links those two episodes together in spite of the nineteen centuries which divide them. A little later, it is stated that "the place was shaken where they were assembled together." Many modern observers of psychic phenomena have testified to vibration of the walls of an apartment, as if a heavy lorry were passing. It is, evidently, to such experiences that Paul alludes when he says: "Our gospel came unto you not in word only, but also in power." The preacher of the New Revelation can most truly say the same words. In connection with the signs of the pentecost, I can most truly say that I have myself experienced them all, the cold sudden wind, the lambent misty flames, all under the mediumship of Mr. Phoenix, an amateur psychic of Glasgow. The fifteen sitters were of one accord upon that occasion, and, by a coincidence, it was in an upper room, at the very top of the house. In a previous section of this essay, I have remarked that no philosophical explanation of these phenomena, known as spiritual, could be conceived which did not show that all, however different in their working, came from the same central source. St. Paul seems to state this in so many words when he says: "But all these worketh that one and the selfsame spirit, dividing to every man severally as he will." Could our modern speculation, forced upon us by the facts, be more tersely stated? He has just enumerated the various gifts, and we find them very close to those of which we have experience. There is first "the word of wisdom," "the word of knowledge" and "faith." All these taken in connection with the Spirit would seem to mean the higher communications from the other side. Then comes healing, which is still practised in certain conditions by a highly virile medium, who has the power of discharging strength, losing just as much as the weakling gains, as instanced by Christ when He said: "Who has touched me? Much virtue" (or power) "has gone out of me." Then we come upon the working of miracles, which we should call the production of phenomena, and which would cover many different types, such as apports, where objects are brought from a distance, levitation of objects or of the human frame into the air, the production of lights and other wonders. Then comes prophecy, which is a real and yet a fitful and often delusive form of mediumship—never so delusive as among the early Christians, who seem all to have mistaken the approaching fall of Jerusalem and the destruction of the Temple, which they could dimly see, as being the end of the world. This mistake is repeated so often and so clearly that it is really not honest to ignore or deny it. Then we come to the power of "discerning the spirits," which corresponds to our clairvoyance, and finally that curious and usually useless gift of tongues, which is also a modern phenomenon. I can remember that some time ago I read the book, "I Heard a Voice," by an eminent barrister, in which he describes how his young daughter began to write Greek fluently with all the complex accents in their correct places. Just after I read it I received a letter from a no less famous physician, who asked my opinion about one of his children who had written a considerable amount of script in mediaeval French. These two recent cases are beyond all doubt, but I have not had convincing evidence of the case where some unintelligible signs drawn by an unlettered man were pronounced by an expert to be in the Ogham or early Celtic character. As the Ogham script is really a combination of straight lines, the latter case may be taken with considerable reserve.

Thus the phenomena associated with the rise of Christianity and those which have appeared during the present spiritual ferment are very analogous. In examining the gifts of the disciples, as mentioned by Matthew and Mark, the only additional point is the raising of the dead. If any of them besides their great leader did in truth rise to this height of power, where life was actually extinct, then he, undoubtedly, far transcended anything which is recorded of modern mediumship. It is clear, however, that such a power must have been very rare, since it would otherwise have been used to revive the bodies of their own martyrs, which does not seem to have been attempted. For Christ the power is clearly admitted, and there are little touches in the description of how it was exercised by Him which are extremely convincing to a psychic student. In the account of how He raised Lazarus from the grave after he had been four days dead— far the most wonderful of all Christ's miracles—it is recorded that as He went down to the graveside He was "groaning." Why was He groaning? No Biblical student seems to have given a satisfactory reason. But anyone who has heard a medium groaning before any great manifestation of power will read into this passage just that touch of practical knowledge, which will convince him of its truth. The miracle, I may add, is none the less wonderful or beyond our human powers, because it was wrought by an extension of natural law, differing only in degree with that which we can ourselves test and even do.

Although our modern manifestations have never attained the power mentioned in the Biblical records, they present some features which are not related in the New Testament. Clairaudience, that is the hearing of a spirit voice, is common to both, but the direct voice, that is the hearing of a voice which all can discern with their material ears, is a well-authenticated phenomenon now which is more rarely mentioned of old. So, too, Spirit-photography, where the camera records what the human eye cannot see, is necessarily a new testimony. Nothing is evidence to those who do not examine evidence, but I can attest most solemnly that I personally know of several cases where the image upon the plate after death has not only been unmistakable, but also has differed entirely from any pre-existing photograph.

As to the methods by which the early Christians communicated with the spirits, or with the "Saints" as they called their dead brethren, we have, so far as I know, no record, though the words of John: "Brothers, believe not every spirit, but try the spirits whether they are of God," show very clearly that spirit communion was a familiar idea, and also that they were plagued, as we are, by the intrusion of unwelcome spiritual elements in their intercourse. Some have conjectured that the "Angel of the Church," who is alluded to in terms which suggest that he was a human being, was really a medium sanctified to the use of that particular congregation. As we have early indications of bishops, deacons and other officials, it is difficult to say what else the "angel" could have been. This, however, must remain a pure speculation. Another speculation which is, perhaps, rather more fruitful is upon what principle did Christ select his twelve chief followers. Out of all the multitudes he chose twelve men. Why these particular ones? It was not for their intelligence or learning, for Peter and John, who were among the most prominent, are expressly described as "unlearned and ignorant men." It was not for their virtue, for one of them proved to be a great villain, and all of them deserted their Master in His need. It was not for their belief, for there were great numbers of believers. And yet it is clear that they were chosen on some principle of selection since they were called in ones and in twos. In at least two cases they were pairs of brothers, as though some family gift or peculiarity, might underlie the choice.

Is it not at least possible that this gift was psychic power, and that Christ, as the greatest exponent who has ever appeared upon earth of that power, desired to surround Himself with others who possessed it to a lesser degree? This He would do for two reasons. The first is that a psychic circle is a great source of strength to one who is himself psychic, as is shown continually in our own experience, where, with a sympathetic and helpful surrounding, an atmosphere is created where all the powers are drawn out. How sensitive Christ was to such an atmosphere is shown by the remark of the Evangelist, that when He visited His own native town, where the townspeople could not take Him seriously, He was unable to do any wonders. The second reason may have been that He desired them to act as His deputies, either during his lifetime or after His death, and that for this reason some natural psychic powers were necessary.

The close connection which appears to exist between the Apostles and the miracles, has been worked out in an interesting fashion by Dr. Abraham Wallace, in his little pamphlet "Jesus of Nazareth."[6] Certainly, no miracle or wonder working, save that of exorcism, is recorded in any of the Evangelists until after the time when Christ began to assemble His circle. Of this circle the three who would appear to have been the most psychic were Peter and the two fellow-fishermen, sons of Zebedee, John and James. These were the three who were summoned when an ideal atmosphere was needed. It will be remembered that when the daughter of Jairus was raised from the dead it was in the presence, and possibly, with the co-operation, of these three assistants. Again, in the case of the Transfiguration, it is impossible to read the account of that wonderful manifestation without being reminded at every turn of one's own spiritual experiences. Here, again, the points are admirably made in "Jesus of Nazareth," and it would be well if that little book, with its scholarly tone, its breadth of treatment and its psychic knowledge, was in the hands of every Biblical student. Dr. Wallace points out that the place, the summit of a hill, was the ideal one for such a manifestation, in its pure air and freedom from interruption; that the drowsy state of the Apostles is paralleled by the members of any circle who are contributing psychic power; that the transfiguring of the face and the shining raiment are known phenomena; above all, that the erection of three altars is meaningless, but that the alternate reading, the erection of three booths or cabinets, one for the medium and one for each materialised form, would absolutely fulfil the most perfect conditions for getting results. This explanation of Wallace's is a remarkable example of a modern brain, with modern knowledge, throwing a clear searchlight across all the centuries and illuminating an incident which has always been obscure.

When we translate Bible language into the terms of modern psychic religion the correspondence becomes evident. It does not take much alteration. Thus for "Lo, a miracle!" we say "This is a manifestation." "The angel of the Lord" becomes "a high spirit." Where we talked of "a voice from heaven," we say "the direct voice." "His eyes were opened and he saw a vision" means "he became clairvoyant." It is only the occultist who can possibly understand the Scriptures as being a real exact record of events.

There are many other small points which seem to bring the story of Christ and of the Apostles into very close touch with modern psychic research, and greatly support the close accuracy of some of the New Testament narrative. One which appeals to me greatly is the action of Christ when He was asked a question which called for a sudden decision, namely the fate of the woman who had been taken in sin.

What did He do? The very last thing that one would have expected or invented. He stooped down before answering and wrote with his finger in the sand. This he did a second time upon a second catch-question being addressed to Him. Can any theologian give a reason for such an action? I hazard the opinion that among the many forms of mediumship which were possessed in the highest form by Christ, was the power of automatic writing, by which He summoned those great forces which were under His control to supply Him with the answer. Granting, as I freely do, that Christ was preternatural, in the sense that He was above and beyond ordinary humanity in His attributes, one may still inquire how far these powers were contained always within His human body, or how far He referred back to spiritual reserves beyond it. When He spoke merely from His human body He was certainly open to error, like the rest of us, for it is recorded how He questioned the woman of Samaria about her husband, to which she replied that she had no husband. In the case of the woman taken in sin, one can only explain His action by the supposition that He opened a channel instantly for the knowledge and wisdom which was preter-human, and which at once gave a decision in favor of large-minded charity. It is interesting to observe the effect which these phenomena, or the report of them, produced upon the orthodox Jews of those days. The greater part obviously discredited them, otherwise they could not have failed to become followers, or at the least to have regarded such a wonder-worker with respect and admiration. One can well imagine how they shook their bearded heads, declared that such occurrences were outside their own experience, and possibly pointed to the local conjuror who earned a few not over-clean denarii by imitating the phenomena. There were others, however, who could not possibly deny, because they either saw or met with witnesses who had seen. These declared roundly that the whole thing was of the devil, drawing from Christ one of those pithy, common-sense arguments in which He excelled. The same two classes of opponents, the scoffers and the diabolists, face us to-day. Verily the old world goes round and so do the events upon its surface. There is one line of thought which may be indicated in the hope that it will find development from the minds and pens of those who have studied most deeply the possibilities of psychic power. It is at least possible, though I admit that under modern conditions it has not been clearly proved, that a medium of great power can charge another with his own force, just as a magnet when rubbed upon a piece of inert steel can turn it also into a magnet. One of the best attested powers of D. D. Home was that he could take burning coals from the fire with impunity and carry them in his hand. He could then—and this comes nearer to the point at issue—place them on the head of anyone who was fearless without their being burned. Spectators have described how the silver filigree of the hair of Mr. Carter Hall used to be gathered over the glowing ember, and Mrs. Hall has mentioned how she combed out the ashes afterwards. Now, in this case, Home was clearly, able to convey, a power to another person, just as Christ, when He was levitated over the lake, was able to convey the same power to Peter, so long as Peter's faith held firm. The question then arises if Home concentrated all his force upon transferring such a power how long would that power last? The experiment was never tried, but it would have borne very, directly upon this argument. For, granting that the power can be transferred, then it is very clear how the Christ circle was able to send forth seventy disciples who were endowed with miraculous functions. It is clear also why, new disciples had to return to Jerusalem to be "baptised of the spirit," to use their phrase, before setting forth upon their wanderings. And when in turn they, desired to send forth representatives would not they lay hands upon them, make passes over them and endeavour to magnetise them in the same way—if that word may express the process? Have we here the meaning of the laying on of hands by the bishop at ordination, a ceremony to which vast importance is still attached, but which may well be the survival of something really vital, the bestowal of the thaumaturgic power? When, at last, through lapse of time or neglect of fresh cultivation, the power ran out, the empty formula may have been carried on, without either the blesser or the blessed understanding what it was that the hands of the bishop, and the force which streamed from them, were meant to bestow. The very words "laying on of hands" would seem to suggest something different from a mere benediction. Enough has been said, perhaps, to show the reader that it is possible to put forward a view of Christ's life which would be in strict accord with the most modern psychic knowledge, and which, far from supplanting Christianity, would show the surprising accuracy of some of the details handed down to us, and would support the novel conclusion that those very miracles, which have been the stumbling block to so many truthful, earnest minds, may finally offer some very cogent arguments for the truth of the whole narrative. Is this then a line of thought which merits the wholesale condemnations and anathemas hurled at it by those who profess to speak in the name of religion? At the same time, though we bring support to the New Testament, it would, indeed, be a misconception if these, or any such remarks, were quoted as sustaining its literal accuracy—an idea from which so much harm has come in the past. It would, indeed, be a good, though an unattainable thing, that a really honest and open-minded attempt should be made to weed out from that record the obvious forgeries and interpolations which disfigure it, and lessen the value of those parts which are really above suspicion.

Is it necessary, for example, to be told, as an inspired fact from Christ's own lips, that Zacharias, the son of Barachias,[7] was struck dead within the precincts of the Temple in the time of Christ, when, by a curious chance, Josephus has independently narrated the incident as having occurred during the siege of Jerusalem, thirty-seven years later? This makes it very clear that this particular Gospel, in its present form, was written after that event, and that the writer fitted into it at least one other incident which had struck his imagination. Unfortunately, a revision by general agreement would be the greatest of all miracles, for two of the very first texts to go would be those which refer to the "Church," an institution and an idea utterly unfamiliar in the days of Christ. Since the object of the insertion of these texts is perfectly clear, there can be no doubt that they are forgeries, but as the whole system of the Papacy rests upon one of them, they are likely to survive for a long time to come. The text alluded to is made further impossible because it is based upon the supposition that Christ and His fishermen conversed together in Latin or Greek, even to the extent of making puns in that language. Surely the want of moral courage and intellectual honesty among Christians will seem as strange to our descendants as it appears marvellous to us that the great thinkers of old could have believed, or at least have pretended to believe, in the fighting sexual deities of Mount Olympus.

Revision is, indeed, needed, and as I have already pleaded, a change of emphasis is also needed, in order to get the grand Christian conception back into the current of reason and progress. The orthodox who, whether from humble faith or some other cause, do not look deeply into such matters, can hardly conceive the stumbling-blocks which are littered about before the feet of their more critical brethren. What is easy, for faith is impossible for reflection. Such expressions as "Saved by the blood of the Lamb" or "Baptised by His precious blood" fill their souls with a gentle and sweet emotion, while upon a more thoughtful mind they have a very different effect. Apart from the apparent injustice of vicarious atonement, the student is well aware that the whole of this sanguinary metaphor is drawn really from the Pagan rites of Mithra, where the neophyte was actually placed under a bull at the ceremony of the TAUROBOLIUM, and was drenched, through a grating, with the blood of the slaughtered animal. Such reminiscences of the more brutal side of Paganism are not helpful to the thoughtful and sensitive modern mind. But what is always fresh and always useful and always beautiful, is the memory of the sweet Spirit who wandered on the hillsides of Galilee; who gathered the children around him; who met his friends in innocent good-fellowship; who shrank from forms and ceremonies, craving always for the inner meaning; who forgave the sinner; who championed the poor, and who in every decision threw his weight upon the side of charity and breadth of view. When to this character you add those wondrous psychic powers already analysed, you do, indeed, find a supreme character in the world's history who obviously stands nearer to the Highest than any other. When one compares the general effect of His teaching with that of the more rigid churches, one marvels how in their dogmatism, their insistence upon forms, their exclusiveness, their pomp and their intolerance, they could have got so far away from the example of their Master, so that as one looks upon Him and them, one feels that there is absolute deep antagonism and that one cannot speak of the Church and Christ, but only of the Church or Christ. And yet every Church produces beautiful souls, though it may be debated whether "produces" or "contains" is the truthful word. We have but to fall back upon our own personal experience if we have lived long and mixed much with our fellow-men. I have myself lived during the seven most impressionable years of my life among Jesuits, the most maligned of all ecclesiastical orders, and I have found them honourable and good men, in all ways estimable outside the narrowness which limits the world to Mother Church. They were athletes, scholars, and gentlemen, nor can I ever remember any examples of that casuistry with which they are reproached. Some of my best friends have been among the parochial clergy of the Church of England, men of sweet and saintly character, whose pecuniary straits were often a scandal and a reproach to the half-hearted folk who accepted their spiritual guidance. I have known, also, splendid men among the Nonconformist clergy, who have often been the champions of liberty, though their views upon that subject have sometimes seemed to contract when one ventured upon their own domain of thought. Each creed has brought out men who were an honour to the human race, and Manning or Shrewsbury, Gordon or Dolling, Booth or Stopford Brooke, are all equally admirable, however diverse the roots from which they grow. Among the great mass of the people, too, there are very many thousands of beautiful souls who have been brought up on the old-fashioned lines, and who never heard of spiritual communion or any other of those matters which have been discussed in these essays, and yet have reached a condition of pure spirituality such as all of us may envy. Who does not know the maiden aunt, the widowed mother, the mellowed elderly man, who live upon the hilltops of unselfishness, shedding kindly thoughts and deeds around them, but with their simple faith deeply, rooted in anything or everything which has come to them in a hereditary fashion with the sanction of some particular authority? I had an aunt who was such an one, and can see her now, worn with austerity and charity, a small, humble figure, creeping to church at all hours from a house which was to her but a waiting-room between services, while she looked at me with sad, wondering, grey eyes. Such people have often reached by instinct, and in spite of dogma, heights, to which no system of philosophy can ever raise us.

But making full allowance for the high products of every creed, which may be only, a proof of the innate goodness of civilised humanity, it is still beyond all doubt that Christianity has broken down, and that this breakdown has been brought home to everyone by the terrible catastrophe which has befallen the world. Can the most optimistic apologist contend that this is a satisfactory, outcome from a religion which has had the unopposed run of Europe for so many centuries? Which has come out of it worst, the Lutheran Prussian, the Catholic Bavarian, or the peoples who have been nurtured by the Greek Church? If we, of the West, have done better, is it not rather an older and higher civilisation and freer political institutions that have held us back from all the cruelties, excesses and immoralities which have taken the world back to the dark ages? It will not do to say that they have occurred in spite of Christianity, and that Christianity is, therefore, not to blame. It is true that Christ's teaching is not to blame, for it is often spoiled in the transmission. But Christianity has taken over control of the morals of Europe, and should have the compelling force which would ensure that those morals would not go to pieces upon the first strain. It is on this point that Christianity must be judged, and the judgment can only be that it has failed. It has not been an active controlling force upon the minds of men. And why? It can only be because there is something essential which is wanting. Men do not take it seriously. Men do not believe in it. Lip service is the only service in innumerable cases, and even lip service grows fainter.

Men, as distinct from women, have, both in the higher and lower classes of life, ceased, in the greater number of cases, to show a living interest in religion. The churches lose their grip upon the people—and lose it rapidly. Small inner circles, convocations, committees, assemblies, meet and debate and pass resolutions of an ever narrower character. But the people go their way and religion is dead, save in so far as intellectual culture and good taste can take its place. But when religion is dead, materialism becomes active, and what active materialism may produce has been seen in Germany. Is it not time, then, for the religious bodies to discourage their own bigots and sectarians, and to seriously consider, if only for self-preservation, how they can get into line once more with that general level of human thought which is now so far in front of them? I say that they can do more than get level—they can lead. But to do so they must, on the one hand, have the firm courage to cut away from their own bodies all that dead tissue which is but a disfigurement and an encumbrance. They must face difficulties of reason, and adapt themselves to the demands of the human intelligence which rejects, and is right in rejecting, much which they offer. Finally, they must gather fresh strength by drawing in all the new truth and all the new power which are afforded by this new wave of inspiration which has been sent into the world by God, and which the human race, deluded and bemused by the would-be clever, has received with such perverse and obstinate incredulity. When they have done all this, they will find not only that they are leading the world with an obvious right to the leadership, but, in addition, that they have come round once more to the very teaching of that Master whom they have so long misrepresented.

Appendix A

DOCTOR GELEY'S EXPERIMENTS

Nothing could be imagined more fantastic and grotesque than the results of the recent experiments of Professor Geley, in France. Before such results the brain, even of the trained psychical student, is dazed, while that of the orthodox man of science, who has given no heed to these developments, is absolutely helpless. In the account of the proceedings which he read lately before the Institut General Psychologique in Paris, on January of last year, Dr. Geley says: "I do not merely say that there has been no fraud; I say, 'there has been no possibility of fraud.' In nearly every case the materialisations were done under my eyes, and I have observed their whole genesis and development." He adds that, in the course of the experiments, more than a hundred experts, mostly doctors, checked the results.

These results may be briefly stated thus. A peculiar whitish matter exuded from the subject, a girl named Eva, coming partly through her skin, partly from her hands, partly from the orifices of her face, especially her mouth. This was photographed repeatedly at every stage of its production, these photographs being appended to the printed treatise. This stuff, solid enough to enable one to touch and to photograph, has been called the ectoplasm. It is a new order of matter, and it is clearly derived from the subject herself, absorbing into her system once more at the end of the experiment. It exudes in such quantities as to entirely, cover her sometimes as with an apron. It is soft and glutinous to the touch, but varies in form and even in colour. Its production causes pain and groans from the subject, and any violence towards it would appear also to affect her. A sudden flash of light, as in a flash-photograph, may or may not cause a retraction of the ectoplasm, but always causes a spasm of the subject. When re-absorbed, it leaves no trace upon the garments through which it has passed.

This is wonderful enough, but far more fantastic is what has still to be told. The most marked property of this ectoplasm, very fully illustrated in the photographs, is that it sets or curdles into the shapes of human members—of fingers, of hands, of faces, which are at first quite sketchy and rudimentary, but rapidly coalesce and develop until they are undistinguishable from those of living beings. Is not this the very strangest and most inexplicable thing that has ever yet been observed by human eyes? These faces or limbs are usually the size of life, but they frequently are quite miniatures. Occasionally they begin by being miniatures, and grow into full size. On their first appearance in the ectoplasm the limb is only on one plane of matter, a mere flat appearance, which rapidly rounds itself off, until it has assumed all three planes and is complete. It may be a mere simulacrum, like a wax hand, or it may be endowed with full power of grasping another hand, with every articulation in perfect working order. The faces which are produced in this amazing way are worthy of study. They do not appear to have represented anyone who has ever been known in life by Doctor Geley.[8] My impression after examining them is that they are much more likely to be within the knowledge of the subject, being girls of the French lower middle class type, such as Eva was, I should imagine, in the habit of meeting. It should be added that Eva herself appears in the photograph as well as the simulacra of humanity. The faces are, on the whole, both pretty and piquant, though of a rather worldly and unrefined type. The latter adjective would not apply to the larger and most elaborate photograph, which represents a very beautiful young woman of a truly spiritual cast of face. Some of the faces are but partially formed, which gives them a grotesque or repellant appearance. What are we to make of such phenomena? There is no use deluding ourselves by the idea that there may be some mistake or some deception. There is neither one nor the other. Apart from the elaborate checks upon these particular results, they correspond closely with those got by Lombroso in Italy, by Schrenk-Notzing in Germany, and by other careful observers. One thing we must bear in mind constantly in considering them, and that is their abnormality. At a liberal estimate, it is not one person in a million who possesses such powers—if a thing which is outside our volition can be described as a power. It is the mechanism of the materialisation medium which has been explored by the acute brain and untiring industry of Doctor Geley, and even presuming, as one may fairly presume, that every materialising medium goes through the same process in order to produce results, still such mediums are exceedingly, rare. Dr. Geley mentions, as an analogous phenomenon on the material side, the presence of dermoid cysts, those mysterious formations, which rise as small tumors in any part of the body, particularly above the eyebrow, and which when opened by the surgeon are found to contain hair, teeth or embryonic bones. There is no doubt, as he claims, some rough analogy, but the dermoid cyst is, at least, in the same flesh and blood plane of nature as the foetus inside it, while in the ectoplasm we are dealing with an entirely new and strange development.

It is not possible to define exactly what occurs in the case of the ectoplasm, nor, on account of its vital connection with the medium and its evanescent nature, has it been separated and subjected to even the roughest chemical analysis which might show whether it is composed of those earthly elements with which we are familiar. Is it rather some coagulation of ether which introduces an absolutely new substance into our world? Such a supposition seems most probable, for a comparison with the analogous substance examined at Dr. Crawford's seances at Belfast, which is at the same time hardly visible to the eye and yet capable of handling a weight of 150 pounds, suggests something entirely new in the way of matter.

But setting aside, as beyond the present speculation, what the exact origin and nature of the ectoplasm may be, it seems to me that there is room for a very suggestive line of thought if we make Geley's experiments the starting point, and lead it in the direction of other manifestations of psycho-material activity. First of all, let us take Crookes' classic experiments with Katie King, a result which for a long time stood alone and isolated but now can be approached by intermittent but definite stages. Thus we can well suppose that during those long periods when Florrie Cook lay in the laboratory in the dark, periods which lasted an hour or more upon some occasions, the ectoplasm was flowing from her as from Eva. Then it was gathering itself into a viscous cloud or pillar close to her frame; then the form of Katie King was evolved from this cloud, in the manner already described, and finally the nexus was broken and the completed body advanced to present itself at the door of communication, showing a person different in every possible attribute save that of sex from the medium, and yet composed wholly or in part from elements extracted from her senseless body. So far, Geley's experiments throw a strong explanatory light upon those of Crookes. And here the Spiritualist must, as it seems to me, be prepared to meet an objection more formidable than the absurd ones of fraud or optical delusion. It is this. If the body of Katie King the spirit is derived from the body of Florrie Cook the psychic, then what assurance have we that the life therein is not really one of the personalities out of which the complex being named Florrie Cook is constructed? It is a thesis which requires careful handling. It is not enough to say that the nature is manifestly superior, for supposing that Florrie Cook represented the average of a number of conflicting personalities, then a single one of these perso-nalities might be far higher than the total effect. Without going deeply into this problem, one can but say that the spirit's own account of its own personality must count for something, and also that an isolated phenomenon must be taken in conjunction with all other psychic phenomena when we are seeking for a correct explanation.

But now let us take this idea of a human being who has the power of emitting a visible substance in which are formed faces which appear to represent distinct individualities, and in extreme cases develop into complete independent human forms. Take this extraordinary fact, and let us see whether, by an extension or modification of this demonstrated process, we may not get some sort of clue as to the modus operandi in other psychic phenomena. It seems to me that we may, at least, obtain indications which amount to a probability, though not to a certainty, as to how some results, hitherto inexplicable, are attained. It is at any rate a provisional speculation, which may suggest a hypothesis for future observers to destroy, modify, or confirm.

The argument which I would advance is this. If a strong materialisation medium can throw out a cloud of stuff which is actually visible, may not a medium of a less pronounced type throw out a similar cloud with analogous properties which is not opaque enough to be seen by the average eye, but can make an impression both on the dry plate in the camera and on the clairvoyant faculty? If that be so—and it would not seem to be a very far-fetched proposition—we have at once an explanation both of psychic photographs and of the visions of the clairvoyant seer. When I say an explanation, I mean of its superficial method of formation, and not of the forces at work behind, which remain no less a mystery even when we accept Dr. Geley's statement that they are "ideoplastic."

Here we have, I think, some attempt at a generalisation, which might, perhaps, be useful in evolving some first signs of order out of this chaos. It is conceivable that the thinner emanation of the clairvoyant would extend far further than the thick material ectoplasm, but have the same property of moulding itself into life, though the life forms would only be visible to the clairvoyant eye. Thus, when Mr. Tom

Tyrrell, or any other competent exponent, stands upon the platform his emanation fills the hall. Into this emanation, as into the visible ectoplasm in Geley's experiments, break the faces and forms of those from the other side who are attracted to the scene by their sympathy with various members of the audience. They are seen and described by Mr. Tyrrell, who with his finely attuned senses, carefully conserved (he hardly eats or drinks upon a day when he demonstrates), can hear that thinner higher voice that calls their names, their old addresses and their messages. So, too, when Mr. Hope and Mrs. Buxton stand with their hands joined over the cap of the camera, they are really throwing out a misty ectoplasm from which the forms loom up which appear upon the photographic plate. It may be that I mistake an analogy for an explanation, but I put the theory on record for what it is worth.

Appendix B

A PARTICULAR INSTANCE

I have been in touch with a series of events in America lately, and can vouch for the facts as much as any man can vouch for facts which did not occur to himself. I have not the least doubt in my own mind that they are true, and a more remarkable double proof of the continuity of life has, I should think, seldom been published. A book has recently been issued by Harpers, of New York, called "The Seven Purposes." In this book the authoress, Miss Margaret Cameron, describes how she suddenly developed the power of automatic writing. She was not a Spiritualist at the time. Her hand was controlled and she wrote a quantity of matter which was entirely outside her own knowledge or character. Upon her doubting whether her sub-conscious self might in some way be producing the writing, which was partly done by planchette, the script was written upside down and from right to left, as though the writer was seated opposite. Such script could not possibly be written by the lady herself. Upon making enquiry as to who was using her hand, the answer came in writing that it was a certain Fred Gaylord, and that his object was to get a message to his mother. The youth was unknown to Miss Cameron, but she knew the family and forwarded the message, with the result that the mother came to see her, examined the evidence, communicated with the son, and finally, returning home, buried all her evidences of mourning, feeling that the boy was no more dead in the old sense than if he were alive in a foreign country.

There is the first proof of preternatural agency, since Miss Cameron developed so much knowledge which she could not have normally acquired, using many phrases and ideas which were characteristic of the deceased. But mark the sequel. Gaylord was merely a pseudonym, as the matter was so private that the real name, which we will put as Bridger, was not disclosed. A few months after the book was published Miss Cameron received a letter from a stranger living a thousand miles away. This letter and the whole correspondence I have seen. The stranger, Mrs. Nicol, says that as a test she would like to ask whether the real name given as Fred Gaylord in the book is not Fred Bridger, as she had psychic reasons for believing so. Miss Cameron replied that it was so, and expressed her great surprise that so secret and private a matter should have been correctly stated. Mrs. Nicol then explained that she and her husband, both connected with journalism and both absolutely agnostic, had discovered that she had the power of automatic writing. That while, using this power she had received communications purporting to come from Fred Bridger whom they had known in life, and that upon reading Miss Cameron's book they had received from Fred Bridger the assurance that he was the same person as the Fred Gaylord of Miss Cameron.

Now, arguing upon these facts, and they would appear most undoubtedly to be facts, what possible answer can the materialist or the sceptic give to the assertion that they are a double proof of the continuity of personality and the possibility of communication? Can any reasonable system of telepathy explain how Miss Cameron discovered the intimate points characteristic of young Gaylord? And then, how are we afterwards, by any possible telepathy, to explain the revelation to Mrs. Nicol of the identity of her communicant, Fred Bridger, with the Fred Gaylord who had been written of by Miss Cameron. The case for return seems to me a very convincing one, though I contend now, as ever, that it is not the return of the lost ones which is of such cogent interest as the message from the beyond which they bear with them.

Appendix C

SPIRIT PHOTOGRAPHY

On this subject I should recommend the reader to consult Coates' "Photographing the Invisible," which states, in a thoughtful and moderate way, the evidence for this most remarkable phase, and illustrates it with many examples. It is pointed out that here, as always, fraud must be carefully guarded against, having been admitted in the case of the French spirit photographer, Buguet.

There are, however, a large number of cases where the photograph, under rigid test conditions in which fraud has been absolutely barred, has reproduced the features of the dead. Here there are limitations and restrictions which call for careful study and observation. These faces of the dead are in some cases as contoured and as recognisable as they were in life, and correspond with no pre-existing picture or photograph. One such case absolutely critic-proof is enough, one would think, to establish survival, and these valid cases are to be counted not in ones, but in hundreds. On the other hand, many of the likenesses, obtained under the same test conditions, are obviously simulacra or pictures built up by some psychic force, not necessarily by the individual spirits themselves, to represent the dead. In some undoubtedly genuine cases it is an exact, or almost exact, reproduction of an existing picture, as if the conscious intelligent force, whatever it might be, had consulted it as to the former appearance of the deceased, and had then built it up in exact accordance with the original. In such cases the spirit face may show as a flat surface instead of a contour. Rigid examination has shown that the existing model was usually outside the ken of the photographer.

Two of the bravest champions whom Spiritualism has ever produced, the late W. T. Stead and the late Archdeacon

Colley—names which will bulk large in days to come—attached great importance to spirit photography as a final and incontestable proof of survival. In his recent work, "Proofs of the Truth of Spiritualism" (Kegan Paul), the eminent botanist, Professor Henslow, has given one case which would really appear to be above criticism. He narrates how the inquirer subjected a sealed packet of plates to the Crewe circle without exposure, endeavoring to get a psychograph. Upon being asked on which plate he desired it, he said "the fifth." Upon this plate being developed, there was found on it a copy of a passage from the Codex Alexandrinus of the New Testament in the British Museum. Reproductions, both of the original and of the copy, will be found in Professor Henslow's book. I have myself been to Crewe and have had results which would be amazing were it not that familiarity blunts the mind to miracles. Three marked plates brought by myself, and handled, developed and fixed by no hand but mine, gave psychic extras. In each case I saw the extra in the negative when it was still wet in the dark room. I reproduce in Plate I a specimen of the results, which is enough in itself to prove the whole case of survival to any reasonable mind. The three sitters are Mr. Oaten, Mr. Walker, and myself, I being obscured by the psychic cloud. In this cloud appears a message of welcome to me from the late Archdeacon Colley. A specimen of the Archdeacon's own handwriting is reproduced in Plate II for the purpose of comparison. Behind, there is an attempt at materialisation obscured by the cloud. The mark on the side of the plate is my identification mark. I trust that I make it clear that no hand but mine ever touched this plate, nor did I ever lose sight of it for a second save when it was in the carrier, which was conveyed straight back to the dark room and there opened. What has any critic to say to that? By the kindness of those fearless pioneers of the movement, Mr. and Mrs. Hewat Mackenzie, I am allowed to publish another example of spirit photography. The circumstances were very remarkable. The visit of the parents to

Crewe was unproductive and their plate a blank save for their own presentment. Returning disappointed, to London they managed, through the mediumship of Mrs. Leonard, to get into touch with their boy, and asked him why they had failed. He replied that the conditions had been bad, but that he had actually succeeded some days later in getting on to the plate of Lady Glenconnor, who had been to Crewe upon a similar errand. The parents communicated with this lady, who replied saying that she had found the image of a stranger upon her plate. On receiving a print they at once recognised their son, and could even see that, as a proof of identity, he had reproduced the bullet wound on his left temple. No. 3 is their gallant son as he appeared in the flesh, No. 4 is his reappearance after death. The opinion of a miniature painter who had done a picture of the young soldier is worth recording as evidence of identity. The artist says: "After painting the miniature of your son Will, I feel I know every turn of his face, and am quite convinced of the likeness of the psychic photograph. All the modelling of the brow, nose and eyes is marked by illness—especially is the mouth slightly contracted—but this does not interfere with the real form. The way the hair grows on the brow and temple is noticeably like the photograph taken before he was wounded."

Appendix D

THE CLAIRVOYANCE OF MRS. B.

At the time of this volume going to press the results obtained by clients of this medium have been forty-two successes out of fifty attempts, checked and docketted by the author. This series forms a most conclusive proof of spirit clairvoyance. An attempt has been made by Mr. E. F. Benson, who examined some of the letters, to explain the results upon the grounds of telepathy. He admits that "The tastes, appearance and character of the deceased are often given, and many names are introduced by the medium, some not traceable, but most of them identical with relations or friends." Such an admission would alone banish thought-reading as an explanation, for there is no evidence in existence to show that this power ever reaches such perfection that one who possesses it could draw the image of a dead man from your brain, fit a correct name to him, and then associate him with all sorts of definite and detailed actions in which he was engaged. Such an explanation is not an explanation but a pretence. But even if one were to allow such a theory to pass, there are numerous incidents in these accounts which could not be explained in such a fashion, where unknown details have been given which were afterwards verified, and even where mistakes in thought upon the part of the sitter were corrected by the medium under spirit guidance. Personally I believe that the medium's own account of how she gets her remarkable results is the absolute truth, and I can imagine no other fashion in which they can be explained. She has, of course, her bad days, and the conditions are always worst when there is an inquisitorial rather than a religious atmosphere in the interview. This intermittent character of the results is, according to my experience, characteristic of spirit clairvoyance as compared with thought-reading, which can, in its more perfect form, become almost automatic within certain marked limits. I may add that the constant practice of some psychical researchers to take no notice at all of the medium's own account of how he or she attains results, but to substitute some complicated and unproved explanation of their own, is as insulting as it is unreasonable. It has been alleged as a slur upon Mrs. B's results and character that she has been twice prosecuted by the police. This is, in fact, not a slur upon the medium but rather upon the law, which is in so barbarous a condition that the true seer fares no better than the impostor, and that no definite psychic principles are recognised. A medium may under such circumstances be a martyr rather than a criminal, and a conviction ceases to be a stain upon the character.

Notes

[←1] "The Reality of Psychic Phenomena." "Experiences in Psychical Science." (Watkins.)

[←2] See Appendix.

[←3] See Appendix D.

[←4] The details of both these latter cases are to be found in "Voices from the Void" by Mrs. Travers Smith, a book containing some well weighed evidence.

[←5] For Geley's Experiments, Appendix A.

[←6] Published at sixpence by the Light Publishing Co., 6, Queen Square, London, W.C. The same firm supplies Dr. Ellis Powell's convincing little book on the same subject.

[←7] The References are to Matthew, xxiii 35, and to Josephus, Wars of the Jews, Book IV, Chapter 5.

[←8] Dr. Geley writes to me that they are unknown either to him or to the medium.

The Singular Existence and Enduring Creations of Sir Arthur Conan Doyle

The man who gave the world the immortal detective Sherlock Holmes and his faithful chronicler Dr. John Watson, Sir Arthur Conan Doyle, was a figure of profound complexity whose life spanned the Victorian and Edwardian eras, mirroring the transformative nature of the period he inhabited, a journey from Edinburgh to the wider world of literature, medicine, and spiritual exploration, born in 1859 into an Irish Catholic family that, despite a distinguished artistic lineage—his father Charles Doyle was an accomplished but troubled artist, succumbing to alcoholism and mental illness, which cast a long shadow over young Arthur's early life—struggled with financial stability, a situation alleviated by wealthy uncles who sponsored his education, notably at Stonyhurst College, a Jesuit preparatory school where he developed a taste for storytelling and a robust physique, both of which would serve him well in later life, subsequently training as a doctor at the University of Edinburgh from 1876 to 1881, a formative experience where he encountered Dr. Joseph Bell, a brilliant surgeon and medical lecturer whose keen powers of observation and deduction would later provide the direct inspiration for the character of Sherlock Holmes, a fact Conan Doyle himself readily acknowledged, remarking on Bell's uncanny ability to diagnose not only a patient's malady but also their profession and recent activities merely by looking at them, a methodology that became the cornerstone of Holmesian genius, the struggling young doctor supplemented his income by writing short stories, a practice he had begun in his late teens, selling his first piece to Chambers's Edinburgh Journal at age nineteen, a nascent literary career that began to flower while he was working as a ship's surgeon on a voyage to the

West African coast and later while establishing an unsuccessful medical practice in Southsea, Portsmouth, a period of professional frustration that ironically gave him the necessary time and quiet to concentrate on his writing, leading to the creation of the detective who would forever overshadow all his other work, the genesis of which was the novella A Study in Scarlet, published in Beeton's Christmas Annual in 1887, introducing the world to the consulting detective and the partnership with Watson that would become the most celebrated duo in literary history, a work followed by The Sign of the Four in 1890, which cemented their popularity, though it was the series of short stories beginning with "A Scandal in Bohemia" in The Strand Magazine in 1891 that transformed Conan Doyle into a literary sensation, the demand for the tales of 221B Baker Street becoming insatiable, to the point where the author felt creatively suffocated by his own creation, viewing the detective fiction as a distraction from his more serious historical novels, which he considered his true literary ambition, works like Micah Clarke (1889), The White Company (1891), and Sir Nigel (1906) demonstrating his considerable skill in the historical genre, a desire for freedom that famously led to the "Great Hiatus" and the apparent death of Holmes at the Reichenbach Falls in the story "The Final Problem" (1893) at the hands of his arch-nemesis Professor Moriarty, a decision that sparked public outcry and even mourning—people wore black armbands—forcing him eventually to resurrect his hero in The Hound of the Baskervilles (1902), a tale set before the fateful duel, and finally bringing him fully back to life in "The Adventure of the Empty House" (1903) with the rather weak explanation that he had merely faked his death, an event that highlighted the immense cultural grip Holmes had achieved, Conan Doyle's life, however, was not solely defined by the Baker Street stories; he was a man of action and diverse interests, serving as a volunteer physician in the Second Boer War, where his experiences led him to write The War in South Africa: Its Cause and Conduct (1900), a pamphlet defending the British actions, for which he received a knighthood in 1902, becoming Sir Arthur Conan Doyle, a recognition that he felt was more for his historical defence of the war than for his literature, he maintained an active interest in justice and famously involved himself in two real-life cases where he helped clear the names of men wrongly convicted: George Edalji and Oscar Slater, using methods reminiscent of his fictional detective to expose miscarriages of justice, further blurring the line between his art and his life, his later years were profoundly shaped by the loss of his first wife, Louise Hawkins, to tuberculosis in 1906, and the devastating impact of World War I, which claimed the lives of his son Kingsley, his brother Innes, two of his nephews, and two brothers-in-law, losses that pushed him deeply into the realm of spiritualism, a cause he championed with fervent devotion from around 1916 until his death, believing in communication with the dead and devoting the remainder of his life to lecturing and writing extensively on the subject, producing works such as The New Revelation (1918) and The History of Spiritualism (1926), often engaging in public debate and controversy over his beliefs, including the notorious affair of the Cottingley Fairies, photographs he championed as genuine evidence of the spiritual world, despite their eventual debunking, a testament to his earnest but sometimes naive pursuit of the supernatural, in addition to the Holmes canon, which spans four novels and fifty-six short stories, and his historical fiction, he also created the formidable character of Professor George Edward Challenger in a series of science fiction stories, including the classic The Lost World (1912), showcasing his versatility and imagination beyond the detective genre, exploring themes of prehistoric life and adventure, a final demonstration of his expansive literary range before his death in 1930 at the age of 71, his legacy remains a towering one in the annals of English literature, not only as the father of the modern detective story, setting the template for forensic investigation and the use of logical deduction that continues to influence crime fiction globally, but also as a complex, multifaceted individual—doctor, historian, soldier, sportsman, and unwavering spiritualist—whose intellectual curiosity and narrative power fundamentally shaped popular culture, ensuring that the brilliant, eccentric tenant of 221B Baker Street and his creator, Sir Arthur Conan Doyle, will be remembered for centuries to come.

Sir Arthur Conan Doyle's Spiritualist Call to the World

Sir Arthur Conan Doyle's The Vital Message, first published in 1919, stands as a profound testament to the author's fervent commitment to Spiritualism, a cause he dedicated a significant portion of his later life and literary output to promoting, seeing it as the most important message for humanity following the catastrophic upheaval of World War I. This non-fiction work serves as a sequel and further elaboration on the concepts introduced in his earlier book, The New Revelation (1918), where he first detailed his conversion to and exploration of spiritualist beliefs. Doyle, an author primarily celebrated for the rational and deductive brilliance of his creation, Sherlock Holmes, paradoxically became one of the world's most outspoken and tireless advocates for the belief system which posits that the spirits of the dead can communicate with the living, primarily through the agency of a medium. He viewed this belief not as a flight of fancy but as a new science and a reformed Christianity, arguing that the evidence gleaned from countless séances and psychic phenomena provided irrefutable proof of an afterlife and the continuity of the soul after bodily death. The Vital Message goes beyond simply stating the case for spiritualism; it is a philosophical and theological treatise that critiques the shortcomings of conventional, institutionalized Christianity, particularly those aspects rooted in what Doyle considered the more primitive and fearful elements of the Old Testament. He champions a more enlightened, practical, and compassionate faith based on the direct, empirically verifiable experiences of Spiritualism, which he believed would usher in an era of greater morality, peace, and understanding among mankind. The book opens with a striking metaphorical comparison, with Doyle looking down from an Alpine pass upon the glorious view of Lombardy, suggesting that a similar "promised land" of spiritual enlightenment awaits humanity if it can but cast off the rigid doctrines and materialist skepticism of the past; he suggests that the Second Coming, long prophesied, may not be a descent of the spiritual to our plane but an ascent of the material to the spiritual, leading to an approximation or even a blending of the two phases of existence. He asserts that the painful lessons learned through the Great War necessitated a deep reevaluation of established religious tenets, claiming that traditional Christian thought had failed to prepare humanity for, or prevent, such an enormous global catastrophe, thus requiring a fresh spiritual foundation. Throughout the volume, Doyle presents what he considers to be the irrefutable evidence for spiritual communication, drawing upon numerous accounts of trance mediumship, direct voice, materializations, and spirit photography, defending these phenomena against the vigorous skepticism and accusations of fraud leveled by critics and established scientific bodies. He discusses the nature of the afterlife, painting a picture of a progression through various spheres of existence, a life of continued learning, atonement, and spiritual development, free from the terrifying, vindictive concepts of eternal damnation propagated by older, fear-based religious teachings. Doyle uses this vision of a benevolent, logical afterlife to deliver his "vital message": that death is not an end but a mere change of condition, that our loved ones who have passed are still near, and that a greater, moral, and rational plan underpins the cosmos, a knowledge which, if universally accepted, would strip away the fear of death and provide a powerful, practical incentive for ethical behavior in life, forming the bedrock for a truly harmonious civilization. This work, along with his other spiritualist writings, demonstrates a powerful shift in Doyle's focus from mere entertainment to a deeply serious, evangelical mission, underscoring his belief that he had a personal responsibility to share this life-altering truth with a world wounded and searching for meaning after the unparalleled suffering of the war. His convictions, passionately articulated in The Vital Message, reveal the earnest and profoundly sincere nature of his commitment to the principles of Spiritualism, a commitment that defined the final decade of his remarkable life.

Arthur Conan Doyle's Spiritual
Synthesis in The Vital Message

Sir Arthur Conan Doyle's The Vital Message, published in 1919, stands as an extraordinary historical document and a deeply personal testament, emerging from the profound historical trauma of the First World War, a period of unprecedented slaughter that had violently shattered the Victorian era's rigid moral and religious certainties and left countless families, including Doyle's own—who had lost his son Kingsley, his brother Innes, and two nephews—desperate for some form of comforting psychological resolution regarding the finality of death, a void which his fervent advocacy of Spiritualism was designed to fill, offering a coherent worldview that could transmute widespread grief and cynical despair into a rationalized hope by asserting the survival of the soul as an empirically verifiable fact. The philosophical undercurrent of this work is a wholesale rejection of the rigid, fear-based theology of orthodox institutionalized Christianity, which Doyle viewed as having failed utterly to prevent the war or to provide genuine, compassionate comfort to its victims; he champions the "New Revelation" of Spiritualism as a superior, modern faith, one founded not on ancient dogma or blind submission, but on a progressive and benevolent cosmology where the afterlife is not a static heaven or a terrifying hell, but a continuous, evolutionary journey through different "spheres of existence," where the soul continues its intellectual and moral development, a concept far more aligned with the scientific and evolutionary thought of the age than the punitive doctrines it sought to replace, thus establishing a pragmatic morality—you behave ethically not from fear of eternal damnation, but from the certain knowledge that your spiritual progress and current state directly affect your life in the next sphere. This commitment to rational justification is where the book engages with the scientific world, or more accurately, attempts to create a new "infant science" of the spirit, as Doyle, the creator of the arch-logician Sherlock Holmes, sought to apply the same deductive rigor to proving the existence of the spirit world that Holmes used to solve crimes, meticulously documenting and defending the phenomena of mediumship, spirit photography, and materialization as evidence that was as tangible and irrefutable as any laboratory experiment, thereby attempting to bridge the seemingly unbridgeable gap between spiritual faith and materialist science, a mission that inevitably placed him in direct, acrimonious conflict with the established scientific community which universally dismissed these findings as either deliberate fraud or the product of self-deception and hysteria, highlighting the deep psychological tension within Doyle himself as he desperately sought to unify his own deeply rational training as a physician and his overwhelming need for spiritual reassurance. Consequently, The Vital Message is not merely a book about Spiritualism; it is a profound psychological document of an era in crisis, providing a comprehensive framework for turning personal tragedy into a universal truth claim, offering the ultimate, soothing message that the dead are "unseen but not absent," still a loving part of the human drama, a philosophical synthesis designed to rebuild a shattered civilization upon the comforting and practical cornerstone of a verifiable, progressive, and endlessly hopeful assurance of life after death.

CONTENTS

Printed in Great Britain
by Amazon